THE BLACK PATCH WAR

THE BLACK PATCH WAR

JOHN G. MILLER

COMMONWEALTH BOOK COMPANY
ST. MARTIN, OHIO

© 1936 by the University of North Carolina Press
© 2021 by Commonwealth Book Company

All rights reserved. No part of this book may be reproduced in any form or by any means without the prior written consent of the publisher, excepting brief quotes used in reviews.
Printed in the United States of America.

ISBN: 978-1-948986-39-7

COMMONWEALTH BOOK COMPANY
St. Martin, Ohio

FOREWORD

IN COMPLIANCE with many requests, I record in the following memoir facts known to me in what may well be called The Black Patch War—an episode in the history of the Black Tobacco Belt of Kentucky and Tennessee.

Of those making requests for the writing of this bit of local history, some participated with me in the scenes described, others witnessed, and still others have no more than hearsay knowledge of them; the great majority have no information yet by hearsay or otherwise of the Black Patch antecedents or of their resultant drama.

To understand and judge rightly the people engaged in this frenzied strife, some knowledge of the social and economic history of this particular section of the country, as far back at least as the Civil War, is necessary. Woodrow Wilson aptly said: "The history of a nation is only the history of its villages [communities] written large."

The source of the train of tragedies of the Night Rider episode lay in the fact that the business, social, and cultural life of the community in the Black Tobacco Belt had long depended almost wholly on the market price of its tobacco.

JOHN G. MILLER

New York, November, 1935

THE REGION known as the Black Tobacco Belt was composed of a number of counties in Western and South Western Kentucky with a considerable portion of adjoining territory in the State of Tennessee. This scope included the cities of Owensboro, Henderson, and Paducah along its northern boundary on the Ohio River, the last named at the mouth of the Tennessee. These with Clarksville, Tennessee, on the Cumberland River, Hopkinsville, and Russellville near, and Guthrie, on the state line, in Kentucky, were important tobacco markets, though not more important than some others nearer the center of the district.

All the places named with numbers not named were involved more or less in the Black Patch War. But the storm struck harder in my native county of Caldwell in Kentucky, and over the counties of Lyon, Trigg, and Christian, and the immediately adjacent part of Tennessee, than elsewhere.

Conditions in the Black Tobacco Belt were in many respects, touching farm life, different from those known in the Burley Tobacco Belt, where there was similar trouble at about the same time. Even with the same character of people, each of the two sections of the state had its own peculiar economic conditions. And it can not be wrong for each to leave to posterity some short and simple annals of its life.

The people of the Black Patch were as nearly homogeneous as any in America, being mainly descendants of the stock from the southern uplands that crossed the

Alleghanies and settled the Cumberland country at the close of the eighteenth and opening of the nineteenth century. They were distinctly an agricultural people, owning small or moderate-sized farms, with here and there holdings large enough to be called plantations. For generations the one crop from which money came was tobacco. "I will pay you when I sell my tobacco," said the debtor to his creditor throughout the black belt. The soil and climate were well suited to a variety of crops. Coal mining began feebly around some parts of this region, and about 1871, the first railroad crossed the counties of Caldwell, Lyon, Livingston, and Marshall while other counties remained years longer without rail connection. Until the close of the century, for unavoidable reasons, resulting to no small extent from the War of the Sixties, the farmer, large or small, in this pocket of the Pennyrile, pinned his hopes to his tobacco money to lift the mortgage from his land and other property; to buy implements and a general outfit for his farm, clothing, groceries, furniture, books and creature comforts for the home; to pay taxes, tuition for his children, dues to the preacher, lawyer, physician, and undertaker, and for modest markers at the graves of his dead. An ordinarily decent appearance among his fellows demanded a good tobacco crop for the individual. A general failure of that crop or a material reduction in its market price meant general disaster— to the owner of the land, the ultimate loss, perhaps, of his home; to the poor tenant family, colored or white, privation and often real suffering. Accustomed to American standards, the free and simple life of the

West, these people were not ready to abide the lower standards of the crowded East. But a more industrious people would have been hard to find. From the well-to-do landowner in the valley, to his share cropper, leading a file of lanky sons from the hills to the field, the toil of each was incessant, often extreme.

In that country the farmer expected in January, usually, a period of ten days or two weeks of bright, warmer weather, with frosty nights, perhaps, but with a sufficient thawing and drying of the ground in the woods for the burning and sowing of plant beds. There might be a recurrence of these "pretty spells" of weather through February and March, during which more beds could be made and sown, so that plants would not all come on at once, but at separate times, thus catching the seasons favorable to setting out tobacco in the spring and early summer. It took a rain to make such a season.

So when the sun shone out, bringing one of these mild intervals in winter—perhaps while the snow still lay along the north side of the fence rows and shaded places—all hands on the farm went to work with might and main to burn the first plantbed. In the woods was selected a spot of rich, loamy soil slanting for drainage, lying fair to the sun, on the south side of a thicket, perhaps; and there dead logs and trash to make sure a quick fire, were mixed with green timber in a huge pile, possibly twenty to thirty feet by fifty to a hundred feet in length. Sometimes two or three days would be consumed in making the heap, combustible material being placed so as to catch the wind, in whatsoever direction it might blow; and at night the torch was applied, and a bonfire would flame high and throw weird gleams and shadows dancing through the woods around. Busy men and boys would attend the fire until late at night to be sure the heap was burning so as to be mainly consumed by morning. Going home with "eyelids heavy and red," they would see the light of neighbors' beds burning far and near. They anxiously studied the air and sky for signs of a change in the weather, because it was important that the bed be dug up and sown before the coming of rain or snow. The following morning, often by dawn, they would be at the plantbed again, working with feverish haste to draw off the remnants of logs only partly consumed, dig up the well-burnt earth, often still hot, into a well-pulverized bed, rake it—carefully removing all roots and lumps—then sow the seeds well mixed with ashes, and, according to the older method, "tramp" and "brush" the bed. To tramp the bed one would start at a corner, and moving sidewise, the width of one of his feet at each advance, would move along one side the length of the bed, and this procedure would be repeated back and forth until the whole bed had been pressed smooth and every seed buried. The bed was then carefully covered with selected brush, laid on uniformly, like shingles on a roof. A later and better method was to cover the bed with a thin, white canvas which would admit sunshine and rain, but afford protection against frost and insects while necessary. As indicated before, all this careful work was repeated from time to time on other beds until April, so that if one bed did not furnish plants of the right size for transplanting at the proper time, another would. The proper time was when a rain would come, anywhere from early in May until June, or, at the utmost, the first days in July.

The land in which the tobacco was to grow was also prepared with great care—was broken, plowed and re-plowed, harrowed and logged to break all clods and to pulverize it—laid off in rows and "checked"; and according to the older way, a hill was made with the hoe precisely in the check. When the ground then was ready for the plants and the plants were ready for the field and rapidly growing too large, how the farmer watched the clouds and prayed for rain! When at last it came, how good it sounded on his roof at night! Up men, women, boys, and girls! Breakfast by candle light! At the plantbeds by dawn! The first basketful —nay, the first bunches of a few hundred plants ready, off to the field; young, supple backs, to set out the plants, row by row. No school for girl or boy that day. Each strong setter followed a boy or girl, or possibly a woman, who carefully dropped each plant in precisely the right place to be set. Scarcely had it fallen from the hand of the dropper before it was seized by the left hand of the setter as his right drove his wooden peg into the earth, making a round hole into which the root of the plant was plunged and deftly set by quick strong fingers which carefully pressed the earth around it. The setter did not take time to straighten up, but as his fingers with the peg gave the quick pressure around the roots of one plant, his left foot went forward toward the next hill, three feet distant, and thus, half bent, he passed from end to end of row after row from early morn till the horn blew or the bell rang for dinner at noon. That meal prepared by such women and girls as were not in the field, was smoking, ready, was quickly swallowed, and the whole force was shortly at work again; some, as before, drawing and carrying plants to those in the field, and the setters still going, half bent, at top speed till nightfall, for it was of utmost importance to take full advantage of this season.—Did backs ache? Oh did they! I remember that once, at the close of such a day of work, a hired man lay down, face foremost, and asked me to stand on his back. My feet were bare. Until I was full grown I dispensed with shoes in this work, as they gathered weight and clogged my feet, while the wet, soft soil was not harsh or hurtful.—A rain following the transplanting assisted the rooting and insured a good stand. The crop was not usually all set at once, but later rains brought later "seasons" and repetitions of the same kind of work.

This description applies to the small farms and farmers—which means the great majority. Upon large plantations, the process might vary slightly from this. But one fact that contributed largely to making tobacco the main money crop was that even upon a small and quite poor farm, where little corn, wheat or other such crop could be raised, very small spots could be found, or could be made, sufficiently fertile to produce a valuable amount of tobacco. It required a small area and was the small farmer's—the poor man's—crop, the hope usually of the tenant and share-cropper, black or white. Often the cropper's wife might request and be allowed a rich spot near the house she occupied, for a patch of tobacco, which she tended as her very own and by which she profited accordingly. It is to be remembered that there and then no railroads, mines, or manufactories furnished accessible markets for other products from the farm.

Even in the small towns and county seats, people kept their cows, pigs and chickens, and cultivated vegetables in their own gardens; and few looked to the farmer for such produce. The few river towns furnished only a limited market to the few farmers in reach, and it was uncertain, usually glutted, and in the hands of a few persons, often one trader, who ready on the bank, had engagements to supply the boats upon their varying and uncertain arrivals.

The same toil and anxious care in setting out the tobacco crop, already described, had to be continued as it grew. It must be plowed several times oftener than other crops, hoed, primed, topped, wormed and suckered, requiring almost constant tending from the transplanting until it was hung in the barn. When a plant was topped—that is, when the bud was nipped out to prevent its flowering and to cause it to spread out large leaves, suckers would sprout where each leaf joined the stalk, all the way to the ground. These must be pulled out from time to time as often as they came, and each one of the eight to twelve leaves on each of the ten to twenty thousand plants, allotted to each laborer, must be lifted up, repeatedly, and the underside scanned for worms and for the eggs of the tobacco fly from which worms were hatched. This care continued through the whole summer, while hot sun rays burnt the laborer's bent, upturned back, and it was often a question whether the farmer or the worms would get most of the crop.

The cutting season lasted from the latter half of August into October, sometimes until late in October, being often determined by the threat of frost. Tobacco cut before it was quite ripe was better than that frost bitten. Very green or badly frost bitten, it was almost or quite worthless. To cut or not to cut was often an anxious question. A threat, or even a slight fall, of frost might prove harmless and be followed by several weeks of bright autumn weather—the finest kind for tobacco. In the late 'sixties and early 'seventies the farmer in the Black Patch had no weather bureau signals for his guidance. But with at least a part of his valuable crop in the fields, he was alert to signs which his father before him had watched—the maturing of certain weeds and seeds, the movements of birds and beasts, a certain eager, nipping of the air; and as late as the middle of September or opening of October, a quick whirl or cut of the wind with a sort of mournful sough from the north—possibly the honk of a wild goose flying southward in the night, would sound a sudden alarm. Up and at it again! In every field in the broad valley, in every hollow between hills where a patch of tobacco stood, knives flashed in the rising sun, went slithering down, splitting each stalk part way to the roots. It was bent to one side, and a deft stroke of the knife in the cutter's strong right hand severed the plant from the ground, and his left set it upside down to "fall"—wilt—so that it could be hung astride a stick or piled in close piles of eight or ten plants each. It would then be shielded largely from the frost in case there was not time or force sufficient to house it that day. Here again the work was fast and furious as at setting time. Men scarcely stopped to eat, as it was important to cut the plants early in the day in time to be wilted in the often faint autumn sunshine. Sometimes, almost the whole outstanding crop in a given section would be cut in a few hours, during which every atom of man power on each farm was worked to its limit.

If any one doubts that housing tobacco is toilsome, let him stand with his feet on tier poles, four feet apart, with no other support, ten, twenty, or thirty feet from the ground floor, and bending down, receive the sticks of heavy tobacco, handed up from below, requiring full use of both hands, then reaching his utmost length, place one stick on the third tier above him, one next below, on down to the poles on which he stands. It may be in late August or early September weather, the heat intense—tobacco on all sides—he bends down and stretches up—down and up—moving backward as the tiers are filled. No fresh air can reach him. Sweat streams from every pore. It stings his eyes. He dares not wipe them. His hands and every thread of cloth in reach are covered with gum that would burn the eye like fire. If he is patient and utters no bad word, count him a saint.

I have never seen in a book or paper a true picture of a field of tobacco in the black belt at its best. Properly the rows were run with almost mathematical precision, the plants being placed all the same distance apart—usually three feet—in as perfect order as squares on a checker board. Under favorable conditions with a good stand and the plants all topped at practically the same time, the leaves would spread so as to leave little earth visible, the top leaves of all the plants about on a level, and, instead of standing up sharp-pointed, as in most illustrations, they went out horizontally, and as they reached ripeness, curved downward, crumpling somewhat, and thick with gum. The farmer wanted it in this state for cutting, and regretted a rain which washed off the gum just as the plant was ready for the knife.

Even though a hailstorm, against which nothing could provide, had not destroyed the crop, and saved from frost, the tobacco had been hung in the barn upon sticks placed at a proper distance apart to prevent "house burning"—a sort of rot from crowding—the tobacco was still to be cured by fire—a highly important but dangerous process. Without great care all the year's labor and hopes might be lost in a flash. Heated, and at a certain stage, a barn of tobacco is almost as inflammable as a tank of oil. If a hot, oily, and partially dried plant or leaf should be allowed to fall upon the fire and flame up, barn and contents might go in a twinkling.

There was little danger when the first fire was lighted, as the tobacco was about as full of sap as when it came off the hill. So the openings and cracks all round the old fashioned barn being closed as far as possible, the lighting of the first fire soon after dark, might be regarded as a sort of festival, and a family, or even neighborly, gathering might celebrate the occasion, the friends bringing supper to the watchman of the night, eating apples, watermelons, and other fruits, chatting by the fire, rejoicing over the crop saved thus far, thinking and hoping more than they ventured to tell of the possibility of a good price and the crop's weighing out well when delivered to the buyer, a few months hence. But work must be done on the morrow, and one person could watch and tend the fire tonight, and he would hear his friends as they chatted and sang snatches of song on their homeward way, and his night's vigil began. The voices died away. The fire that had flashed bright in the beginning, had sunk to a steady glow, and must be kept at that—hot but not flaming up. There was no chance to read. The slow fires flickered and sputtered and the watcher sat and thought in silence, and, save when replenishing the fires, in absolute stillness the long night through. On some nights, when the sky was clear and frost was in the air, the only sound to be heard was the strange ch-e-ir-ar of the redheaded woodpecker, falling through the silence, now and then, as he went his southward way. It seemed to inquire, not noisily but anxiously, if any other redhead might be in hearing. After a short but appreciable interval, an answer would come from perhaps the west, followed by a like interval, then an answer from the east, then a hail faintly heard far behind, and by that time the first voice replying from far in the south could scarcely be heard. It would seem that the whole kinship of redheads—each on his own initiative—had decided to go south on that night. For soon the calls and answers were numerous and widespread, but all so cautious and separate as to indicate a desire to move with no more noise than was necessary for each to report occasionally his whereabouts and safety on the way. There was a weird loneliness in the call not to be forgotten. I have wondered why I have never seen any mention of it in bird lover's books. And I wonder if redheads are flying with their cautious hail on chilly autumn nights, over the Kentucky Pennyrile, as they were in the fall of seventy-three.

As many times as every plant and every leaf of the crop had been handled up to the time it was housed, every plant and every leaf was to be handled after it was cured, again and again, and separately, in the sorting, stripping and tying, bulking and often rebulking and rehanging, until it was finally sold in the next winter, or even the next spring, after plantbeds had been sown and work begun upon a tobacco crop for the following year—two crops on hand at one and the same time.

From 1865 to 1873, Kentuckians had been struggling out of the wreckage left by the Civil War. In the latter year, a good general crop and an unusually good tobacco crop had been produced. There were indications that the vast streams of capital which had poured from centers of wealth upon northwestern railroads and other enterprises, north of the Mason-Dixon line, might send at least some overflow southward. Hope revived. But in September, 1873, came the Jay Cooke & Company failure with panic in its wake. To the farmer facing ruin in the tobacco belt the future looked black. In 1874, marching side by side with the awful, almost unprecedented, drought, came the devastating hordes of "army worms" and "chinch bugs." For want of seasons for planting, the tobacco crop was an utter failure.

Corn, riddled by the insect pests and scorched by heat and drouth, withered on the hill. Rich grass and clover fields, green in early spring, by midsummer were brown; and cattle searching pastures only stirred clouds of dust. Wheat saved from a partially good and earlier crop must be fed to horses, cattle, and hogs.

But the good crops of 1873 with the proceeds of the tobacco sold in the winter and spring of 1874, though at lower prices than had been hoped for, helped to bridge over the time of scarcity. The next season was far more favorable for crops. The citizen of this section, relying upon his individual efforts and resources, asked no governmental favors but only an equal chance with his fellow countrymen, and his energy did not flag. In the face of bankruptcies, market failures, economic changes, and fluctuations of finance in national and banking circles, organizations such as the "Grangers" had been formed and farmers began to search for and discuss the causes of some of their ills. Still tobacco stood as the main dependence for ready cash. But monopoly of its market was yet almost unknown. It was open to all dealers alike.

The railroad, though built by oppressive taxation, voted by a majority eager for transportation lines, had nevertheless increased facilities for moving crops. Every little railway station afforded an opportunity for a warehouse. Competition among traders was keen, and even "off the railroad" small "tobacco factories," as they were called, dotted the whole tobacco belt, bringing the market almost to the farmer's barn door, and establishing this product more firmly than ever as King of Staples.

Though I had left the farm about 1874, and, for a quarter of a century had been absorbed in other interests, I had continued to pass to and fro in the Pennyrile and had casually—and only casually—observed these conditions. About the close of the century it began to be noticeable that different warehouses and trading places stood closed and deserted. I had but a hazy, if any, idea of the cause of this change. Between 1900 and 1906 I had occasion to be in Eddyville, Lyon County, Kentucky, and saw one day in the familiar old court room, a considerable assembly of farmers engaged in a heated discussion between what seemed to be opposing factions over the policy of some farmers' association for control of the tobacco market. I had no definite conception of the issue in dispute but silently sympathized with the effort that had farm relief for its object.

The cause of the closing of many warehouses and trading places that had been active previously, was, of course, the rapid rise of what was commonly known as the "Tobacco Trust." How governments in Europe monopolized the tobacco markets in their respective domains, and how imperial capitalistic agencies were established on both sides of the Atlantic, and how, operating jointly, they cornered the market on both continents, finally came to be fairly well understood both by those who produced and by those who traded in tobacco.

These powerful combinations acting in concert fixed arbitrary prices for all classes and grades of tobacco. Each particular European market had its agents, or representatives, in America. The independent buyer in the tobacco belt must dispose of his purchase through these agencies and at their prices or let it rot on his hands. He was soon driven from the field. At a place like Princeton, Caldwell County, for example, there were the agencies of two great companies. It was said with every appearance of truth that between them they would divide the county into geographical districts with an agreement that neither would, in purchasing certain tobaccos, encroach upon the territory of the other, nor in his own section pay more than an agreed price for a given grade of leaf or lugs. A farmer on the west side of the Fredonia Road, say, might decline a most unreasonable offer for his tobacco and wait for the buyer's competitor; but such competition would not come. Another buyer might come, but it would be merely to say he could offer no more. The producer was at the mercy of the speculator, and many tobacco raisers were steadily facing ruin, and as a class were approaching economic serfdom.

No doubt about the wrong. What could be the remedy? No attempt will be made here to point out the remedy. I am simply trying to tell what actually occurred. Surely, lawlessness could not right the wrong. But men differed as to the wise course. Feeling was deep. Men's families were suffering. Secret meetings began. What was commonly known as The Black Tobacco Association had been formed with a plan for pooling all the tobacco, advancing a part of the value under a grading system, and holding the entire crop until purchasers would be forced to pay more. This roughly states the main idea of the plan for retaliation. Many doubted the feasibility of the plan, and declined to adhere to it. It was of course opposed by the Trusts and their friends.

On some occasions upon visiting my old county town, Princeton, I was conscious of a constrained and anxious air, and caught hints of impending evil and of vague threats—tension in the social atmosphere and apprehension on the faces of thoughtful men. Reports came of lawless acts in other localities. But it seemed impossible that such things could come to the orderly community which one had known so long, and which even the stress and strain and fiercely divided sentiment of the Civil War had not driven to lawlessness. Still disturbing reports of outbreaks in more or less remote places continued to appear in the press. On a railroad train, passing through certain sections, conversations between men and women would be heard manifesting deep though somewhat repressed emotion and divided sentiment. In one of these discussions, I overheard for the first time that I can recall, the term "Night Riders"; and that organization was being stoutly defended by one of the women passengers. It seemed to be considered a part of The Black Tobacco Association or connected with that body.

As yet Paducah and some of the larger towns seemed to be immune to the spirit of unrest. But upon reaching my office one morning in 1906, I found one of my partners already there. He had begun no work and in answer to my usual salutation, he said: "I learn a body of men, armed and masked, raided Princeton last night, shot up the town, took charge of telephone lines, drove people off the streets, ordering them to remain indoors, burned the two large tobacco warehouses there with all their contents, terrifying the whole community, threatening death to any who might oppose their course."

This man as well as I had been reared in Caldwell County, and I said to him that I could not believe the people of our native county could be guilty of making such a lawless raid upon their county seat and that that mob must have been formed elsewhere. But to this, he made no reply. He had lived there more recently than I had and was better informed as to conditions in some parts of the county.

I had in mind the people of the rather more prosperous and orderly Fredonia Valley in the northwest portion of the county—including the staid Bethlehem Presbyterian Church neighborhood—my former habitat. This community while bitterly opposed to the Trusts, was equally opposed to lawlessness of any degree or of any kind as a means of redress. From them many of the people in the adjacent part of the Knob district, on the north side of the county of Caldwell, took their tone, and all were nicknamed "Hill Billies." But among a very large element in other parts of the whole black tobacco country, patience had ceased to be a virtue. They had been wronged and they knew it. They had suffered long and looked in vain for help. Women and children were threatened with want. This party had formed an Association for relief. It tolerated no plan but its own. Its members resolved that they would not and others should not sell to the Trust—nor to nor through any agency other than the Association with its branches. They took the law into their own hands. Those who would not pool their tobacco must be forced to do so even under the lash upon their bare backs, resistance to which meant death.

Meetings were held on public days in the county seats and elsewhere. Great throngs with tense nerves, sweat dropping from knotted brows, in excitement too deep for applause, listened with bated breath to impassioned speakers, some fiercely fanatical, some artful and designing, as they pictured the toil and servitude of the farmer in contrast with the ease and luxury of his lord and master, the purse-proud capitalist. All the changes were rung upon such things as the Boston Tea Party, and every well-known instance of resistance to tyranny was cited as a precedent justifying extreme measures regardless of law. Nothing that could appeal to prejudice or play upon passion was left untried.

This is no fanciful picture. I have seen just such gatherings. And it was surprising to note the character of some of those who would make such arguments. In the midst of this episode and some of its incidents to be set forth later, a circuit judge, who was off the bench only for his noonday meal, in private conversation with me, defended the worst of the Night Rider outrages and cited the Boston Tea Party as a justifying precedent.

Anyone who bought or sold tobacco independently of the Association was doomed. The Trust left the independent buyer's purchased tobacco to rot on his hands. The Night Rider burnt his warehouse and his purchase with it, and whipped him, and if he resisted, slew him. To destroy the warehouses, the great receiving plants of the Trust, would leave all tobacco raisers to sell to the Association or lose their crops. Hence to burn a Trust warehouse was a noble act. Force the Trust out of the market. To destroy one monopoly another was to be set up and supported by violence. Such seemed to be the policy followed.

In schoolrooms and vacant houses, meetings were held for the initiation and training of members, with "grips," signals, and countersigns, under officers known as captains, colonels of the "Silent Brigade," bound by solemn oaths to secrecy, to obey the commands of the chosen leaders and do the will, and execute the orders of the majority.

Large warehouses with great stores of tobacco, railroad station buildings and other property were destroyed by fire, far and wide; farmhouses and barns of nonmembers were burned, men and women whipped and sometimes murdered in their homes. If one dared to criticize, his property and his life were in danger. On one occasion a man named Henry Bennett, a farmer and trader of the vicinity of Dycusburg, Crittenden County, Kentucky, being in Eddyville, county seat of Lyon, and perhaps under the influence of liquor, made remarks derogatory to the Night Riders and their methods. No outbreaks of consequence had occurred in his immediate vicinity, and he may have felt that the bands might not come where they had no known lodges. But on the first or second night following his remarks in Eddyville, a band on horseback was seen on the old turnpike in Caldwell County, more than twenty miles from Dycusburg. It was augmented as it approached

Eddyville, through which it was seen to pass like a group of specters, still fourteen miles from its destination. Wake Bennett! They are coming! Silent but swift, they soon arrive, and Bennett wakes to find his quiet home surrounded by armed men. Helpless, and in the presence of his frightened family, he is hurried out to a tree by his front door, his shirt torn from his body, his arms drawn round the tree and held while his bare back is lashed with a thorn branch till the blood runs in streams, and a part of one ear cut off. And he is ordered to keep silent in future or to expect even worse. Before daybreak, the band passes back through Eddyville in the direction of the locality from which it came. Bennett fled his home. His offense had been the exercise of free speech against Night Rider methods.

At another time the village of Fredonia, twelve miles north of Princeton, wakened in the night to find itself a captive. Telephone? Every wire had been cut, and the flames of Rice Brothers' large tobacco warehouse with its contents lit up the night. In the same way the tobacco warehouse of Carden, a buyer in Crittenden County, a little farther from Princeton, was soon afterward surrounded at night by an armed band, and with its contents reduced to ashes. In places such as these, where the organization was not strong, greater caution was exercised than in outrages in Night Rider hotbeds—such as some localities in the southern part of Caldwell and Lyon counties and adjacent parts of Trigg and Christian counties. In the latter sections, a stranger passing about in the neighborhood without a convincing explanation of his business was in danger of such treatment as might be suffered by one suspected of being a revenue officer in a moonshiner district.

A young county attorney, not at all robust, who attempted some futile efforts to discharge his official duty, as against this lawlessness, was openly assaulted and beaten by a stalwart member of the Silent Brigade on the streets of Eddyville, the Lyon County seat. The point was soon reached when anyone whose conduct about anything displeased certain leaders of the organization was in danger, however neutral he might be toward the opposing factions. The police judge of the town of Eddyville, for some mysterious reason, was taken out and whipped. He fled the town. An humble hack driver of the same place received similar Night Rider discipline. The home of a family of negroes at Birmingham on the Tennessee River in the edge of Marshall County, Kentucky, was surrounded at night by men from that county and Lyon County, and destroyed, and some of the inmates murdered.

One whose testimony as a witness was feared, might mysteriously disappear and be seen no more. Men were shot down in their homes or wounded by secretly placed bombs. Plantbeds belonging to Hill Billies were destroyed.

At last retaliation began, and plantbeds belonging to members of the Association, it is said, were destroyed. It was said that some individuals sent direct warning to prominent Night Rider champions that they would be held personally responsible and receive severe treatment in return for injury done to the sender of the message or to designated friends by any Night Rider whomsoever. But these were rare instances—if such things occurred. No organized bands of Hill Billies went forth—not one barn was burnt, not one home attacked, nor one man or woman whipped, assaulted, or disturbed in his home by organized Hill Billie bands.

The one faction was organized for aggressive action. The other was not. As already seen the Night Riders were an oathbound order for an express purpose, secretly commanded, and after military fashion, drilled in a system of tactics to execute its designs. Their real name, "Silent Brigade," was a secret, and part of a password until exposed as will be later shown.

The outspoken theory and purpose of those who insisted upon obedience to law was opposition to organized lawlessness, and to them organization to retaliate was therefore impossible. They could look only to the orderly processes of government and, though their opponents were really in the minority in the Black Patch, that minority was in practically entire control of the legal machinery—the courts and officers of the counties and judicial districts; and these county and district governments, outside of the condition I shall presently point out, were practically, at that time, independent of the State's Executive.

It was a time that tested not only the physical and moral courage but the mental poise of genuinely good men. The specious arguments and the appeals to passion and self-interest had led men of good character, church members and pillars of some communities, to engage in or approve and applaud conduct at which under ordinary conditions a short time previously they would have been appalled. The secret and mysterious rituals, the regalia and military formations, the swift and silent rides with arms at night into strange neighborhoods to attack an alleged foe in the enemy's country, the opportunities for leadership, with the high-sounding titles and authority of office, in many cases the opportunity to gratify a spirit of revenge and spite, called not only the young and thoughtless, but the evil-minded and vicious into an oath-bound organization which could boast that it "feared no judge nor jury," but which controlled the courts, distributed political favors and dominated the social and material interests of the community. Once drawn or even coerced into such an organization and participating unexpectedly or even unwillingly in its wrongdoing, a man would thereafter be at the mercy of its most unscrupulous members. The relationship between the ordinary county town, such as Princeton, and the farming interests was so close, that a large part of the citizenship of the town, merchants, bankers, industrial workers, profession men, and others looking to rural patronage, became stockholders in the Association whose auxiliary and main reliance was the Silent Brigade. A prosperous farmer in a Night Rider neighborhood would be told significantly that he was expected to invest a certain amount in stock of the Black Tobacco Association. Though he might be utterly averse to the investment, he would think of the Silent Brigade, which he did not then know by that name, and his course of action could be described in the words of one to me, "I took the stock." Not only did the majority of the county officers and also of the members of the county bar belong to the Association, but many of them had taken the Night Rider oath—were members of the "inner circle"—and were instructed in its ritual and familiar with its secret signs and signals. Such a thing as a grand or petit jury, free from the dominion of the Association in the courts of the state in this region, was an impossibility. I had evidence which was reliable, describing in part at least, the system of signals for use when necessary between counsel and jury during the progress of a trial. A circuit judge would deliver to a grand jury a solemn charge for law enforcement, often loudly applauded in the press, but in reality a solemn farce. For the judge believed and the jury knew it would not be obeyed to the detriment of Night Rider bands. The Black Tobacco Association ruled the county government by virtue of the Silent Brigade.

In the southern part of Caldwell County, Kentucky, in the midst of a Night Rider hotbed, lived Robert L. Hollowell, his wife, Mary Lou, and their only child, a thirteen-year-old boy, Price. They raised tobacco but despite all persuasion and threat declined to join the Association or pool their crop. While Robert Hollowell was mild-mannered and inclined for the sake of peace to submit even to insult, Mary Lou was high-spirited and likely to express her opinion with freedom. Her father in his lifetime had been a teacher and she had been well-reared—certainly as well as the average woman of that community. She had formerly lived and conducted some sort of business in Princeton, dressed well, was tall and well-formed, made a handsome appearance and had associates in the towns. Her brother, a prosperous farmer a few miles away, also stood aloof from the Association. In the spring of 1907, the plantbeds of Robert Hollowell and his brother-in-law, Eastland, were "scraped" and destroyed by unknown hands. An act had recently been passed by the state legislature making such an offense felonious—punishable by confinement in the penitentiary—but to convict a Night Rider of scraping a plantbed was as difficult as it was to convict him for burning a factory or murdering a Hill Billie—impossible. But it was not impossible for Mary Lou to express her opinion of the perpetration of the outrage, and perhaps, to make an effort to have him apprehended. Feeling rose to fever heat, and she was herself accused of scraping a plantbed or of having it done, as will presently appear. Hatred toward her was intense.

One quiet night in May or June, 1907, this family of three was awakened by the sound of firearms, and a storm of bullets crashed through windows and doors and into the walls and roof, and from different sides the command was heard, "Close up, men, close up." The three sprang out of their beds and dodged under them or into whatever place seemed safest, the mother first grasping her boy. The assailants did close up with oaths and abusive words. The victims were dragged out. Mary Lou, slightly wounded by a gunshot, was kicked by a well-known young man of the vicinity. Bob was led out, his back, laid bare, was lashed with a whip till the blood ran down, his arms held and drawn forward, while the whip was wielded by a highly respected member of the community, a pillar in the Baptist church. The assailants boasted, "We fear no judge nor jury," and a woman member of the band exclaimed, "This is sweet revenge to me."

The victims were left to writhe the remainder of the night, their last night together in this shattered home. After Hollowell's aged mother, living near by, had seen and tried to soothe his lacerated back on the following morning, Bob bade her goodbye to see her no more, and with his wife and son left his farm and what was on it forever. Perhaps his horses with some other personal property were salvaged, but his crop of wheat, corn and other things went to waste and sheep, hogs, and cattle were taken by whomsoever might, for it would have been a brave man who would at that juncture have dared to take charge of these and the deserted home without permission of its despoilers. It is easy to see how poor was Hollowell's chance to sell that farm for its real worth. After some slight medical treatment at Princeton, the family fled to Paducah for temporary refuge.

In the early spring, a plantbed of a neighbor of the Hollowell's had been scraped, as it was alleged, and a grand jury by a majority vote indicted, not Bob, but Mary Lou Hollowell, for this offense. While it was well known that she was in Paducah, McCracken County, Kentucky, only forty-six miles distant, the simple and customary process, a writ directed to the sheriff of McCracken for her arrest and return to Caldwell County for trial, was not adopted till long afterward. The reason for this will soon appear.

THE BLACK PATCH WAR

While I had long known of the large Hollowell family in Caldwell and Lyon counties, and had met casually one or two of its members, I had never, so far as I could recall, even heard of Robert Hollowell nor of his wife. But the latter had known one of the members of our firm, and immediately upon arriving in Paducah, sought through him to engage us as legal counsel to obtain redress. By mere coincidence, I was called to Princeton on entirely different business on that or the following day, and while there learned that the seemingly incredible story was true, and that whoever had perpetrated the outrage, its enormity had been in no respect overtold in the report made to my partner.

One of the county officers, the sheriff, seemed at that time not to have entered Night Rider ranks, and he had gone, perhaps at Hollowell's request to bring away some horses left on the farm, and had seen the ruined home. An old schoolmate of mine in Princeton, knowing the facts, said to me:

"Johnnie, there stands the house, riddled by bullets, windows and doors smashed, fences broken, stock wandering at will through the unguarded, growing crop. Bob and his family, usually industrious and careful, gone and not daring to come back even to see his old sick mother in her home close to his."

On the day Mary Lou Hollowell left Princeton for Paducah, feeling was so fierce against her that it was thought necessary to escort her to the railroad train with a guard. On this visit to Princeton, I discovered that her private character would be assailed should she seek redress. Her husband was in less danger than she and had waited there to dispose quietly of some details before leaving the town also. He was pointed out to me as friends accompanied him to the railway station. Returning to Paducah my seat on the train was near his. He seemed to wear the look of a stunned person and a fugitive, going with his young son he knew not where.

In a final, private conference on the subject, sometime later, both of my partners expressed their unwillingness to engage in the prosecution of a civil action in behalf of the Hollowells against the parties they named for damages, not, as I understood, because they thought the claim to be ill-founded, but one was about to become a candidate for a state office and the other had property and business interests in Caldwell County that would be endangered by his appearance as attorney for plaintiffs in such action. Both those partners, however, were willing to engage in defending Mrs. Hollowell against the charge of scraping a plantbed, as made in the indictment which had been found, if same should be actually pressed for trial. Their main reliance even in that matter would be ultimately a pardon by the governor of the state. They well understood such civil action for damages by any of the Hollowells, as well as any defense against the indictment, in the Caldwell Circuit Court at that time would be futile.

There was during that period in Kentucky no statewide constabulary. Each county was a separate unit, under a separate government with which the state executive could not interfere for the suppression of lawlessness without a request from the county authorities.

These lawyers doubtless considered the circuit judge and the commonwealth's attorney in that judicial district powerless in the presence of organized outlawry. All the partners understood and appreciated the danger to property, to political prospects, and even to life that must be faced by a lawyer bringing a civil suit of the kind contemplated against the parties whom our clients accused. But the reader may guess one's feeling at the thought that such an outrage should have been perpetrated in Kentucky and that the victims could find no lawyer who would dare to bring their suits for damages against those they had with evident sincerity and strong corroboration pointed out as their actual assailants. Our partnership was to be dissolved a few months hence; and, resolved to bide my time, I said little but thought that a court and a jury might be invoked which even Caldwell and Lyon County Night Riders could learn to fear. Such an idea did not occur to my partners or, if it did, they were still unwilling to make the test, as will soon appear.

Though I had never seen Mary Lou Hollowell previously, when this decision was reached by our firm, the management of her defense fell into my hands, and afterward in a conference she appealed with intense emotion to me personally to take charge of the claims of herself and family for civil damages also. I told her the decision of the firm was irrevocable though we sympathized with her and her family in their distress, and that it was highly important for me to know with absolute certainty what connection, if any, she directly or indirectly, may have had with the commission of the offense charged in the indictment; that she might confess everything to me as her counsel and that I would not, and under the law, could not be forced to violate her confidence in this respect, and that even if she was to any extent involved, a full confession of all she knew about the alleged offense, might be of the utmost importance to her and her family. To my astonishment, she fell upon her knees, held up her right hand and said: "I swear to you that I had nothing to do with the scraping of that plantbed, have no knowledge of who did it and am as innocent of that charge as an unborn child—so help me, God!"

Then, requiring a promise of secrecy, I told her that after a certain designated date within a few months, I should feel free to accept, if she still so desired, an employment in the damage suits, but upon conditions to be then stated and without which the arrangement could not be made. Robert Hollowell had secured employment in Paducah. For a time he had gone with his family to Oklahoma, but on account of the strain upon his system, his nervous and mental condition was such his wife was advised it would be wise to yield to his wish to return to his native state, and they had come back to Paducah.

At length my previous partnership became dissolved, and I explained at the proper time that our recently formed firm of Miller & Miller would undertake to recover damages for the Hollowells only upon condition that they in good faith establish a residence in some state other than Kentucky. After the husband had had steady occupation for a time and seemed in better condition, they moved to Evansville, Indiana, where he obtained similar employment.

My son, John Goodrum Miller, Jr., graduating from the Law Department of Centre College in 1906, had been admitted to the bar—hence the new firm just mentioned. Our purpose was to cause a diversity of citizenship that would give the federal court jurisdiction of a civil action of our clients against citizens of Kentucky, who had assaulted them—a plan which seemed to have occurred to none of the many who throughout the state had been seeking some means by which to check the torrent of lawlessness.

The terms of the federal court in Paducah where we must bring the suits, were held in November and April of each year. Before our clients were definitely settled in Evansville, the term for November had passed and that for April, 1908, was not far ahead. Not much time was to be lost if the twenty-eight or thirty defendants, recognized by our clients in the attacking band, were to be found in different counties and summoned for the coming April term. In the beginning, Mary Lou alone was informed of the plan, but she and Bob also, after he learned it, guarded the secret well, and when the refugees moved to Indiana no Night Rider dreamed of danger from that quarter.

Early in 1908, a curious and what proved to be a difficult complication arose. Late one afternoon near the end of January, a telegram from a gentleman, then president of the First National Bank of Princeton, asked me to meet him at the Palmer House in Paducah immediately after the arrival of the six o'clock afternoon train from Princeton. I knew that the Hollowells, especially in the beginning of their troubles, considered this man their close friend, and I naturally thought it barely possible that his visit might relate to their affairs. Not so. Another matter entirely, equally delicate and important, and as it proved really more difficult, was involved. But I was cautious, and the Hollowell matters were not named. To my amazement it turned out that some promoters and "plungers" in mining and realty ventures had involved him in large sums and that he faced disaster. I had known him from the time he was eight or ten years of age, attending one of my country schools, and observing his growing agitation when we were in the hotel dining room, I suggested that we go at once to our law office. He asked me if one of my former partners did not still have a room in our suite, stating that he did not want to be seen there by this gentleman, who was a stockholder in the bank of which he was president. He was exceedingly anxious that no stockholder and certainly no director of his bank should have the slightest inkling of these ventures and his personal entanglements, though they did not involve the bank in the sum of a single cent. Though a seasoned and hardened business man, he walked the floor of our office, wringing his hands in great distress during the conference.

The deposits in his bank, one of the strongest in our part of the state, came largely from the southern part of Caldwell County. It was practically a Tobacco Association bank, and members of that organization were on its directory; and leaders of the Silent Brigade, who but for this fact, seldom would have been seen there, were familiar figures in its lobby.

So the law firm of Miller & Miller, only partially aware of all this, were, while in charge of the matters of this banker and of those of the Hollowells at once, almost in the situation of one walking in darkness with a stick of dynamite in each hand. It was important to extricate the banker from his entanglement, if possible, by some adjustment or maneuver that would avoid the publicity of litigation—especially in his own county. A slight blunder might cause collision and explosion. It is not possible to explain all the complications and narrow escapes without making the story too long. But during the winter, a number of trips were made on the banker client's business, to Madisonville in Hopkins County, Greenville in Muhlenburg County, Princeton in Caldwell County, and elsewhere, during which I met continually those whom I understood to be Night Riders, some of them spotted as the Hollowells' assailants. The banker was greatly concerned that all these should know nothing of my business with him, and I was equally concerned for reasons of which he was totally ignorant. Eminent lawyers of Madisonville, Kentucky, represented his adversaries.

Late in February, a private meeting was arranged at the Henrietta Hotel in Princeton. The leader of opposing counsel and some of his clients were to come on the afternoon train, on a day named, to meet us there, but telephoned from Nortonville of some mishap on the way and failed to meet us, and we returned to Paducah. People, their nerves already tense, had seen enough to awaken suspicion, in the small town, of some mysterious business in our hands for the prominent president of the largest bank. Night Riders were keenly alert, some of them dubious of his loyalty to their cause; but, ignorant of danger from the federal court, still "feared no judge nor jury."

After our pleadings in the Hollowell cases were fully prepared but before the suits were instituted, remembering that that business had first come to the former firm, though both my former partners had definitely declined it, we wanted them to have another opportunity to accept or decline the employment. In fact, we would have welcomed their help. The campaign in which one of them had been interested had passed and he was apparently out of politics. Upon invitation they came to our office for conference. In strictest confidence our plans were outlined for instituting the civil suits for the Hollowells; they were told that the pleadings had been prepared for filing in the United States court, and they were invited to assist in the litigation. Both declined. In view of the danger involved, both agreed to keep the facts secret till after the actions had been instituted. This occurred only a few days prior to the trip to Princeton to meet counsel from Madisonville in the effort, as before told, to adjust the matters of our banker client. For more reasons than have been explained here, it was highly desirable to make that settlement, if possible, prior to the filing of the Hollowell suits.

On the morning following our abortive trips to Princeton, our client there telephoned me in Paducah, saying in a highly excited voice that the regular local attorney for the Black Tobacco Association at Princeton had, just that morning, called at his office, stating that suits were about to be begun by the Hollowells at Paducah against Caldwell County persons, and charging him as the instigator of those suits. He said the information had come in a letter written on the day previous by the lawyer who on that day was to have met us in Princeton and failed to do so. Calming as best I could the client's fears, I promised to call this Madisonville lawyer by wire, and to demand his authority for the statement and to clear him—our client—of the charge.

This lawyer was called at once and answered somewhat evasively, failing to name any authority but saying it was a rumor in his town that some one with some such name as "Holloman" had suit prepared in Paducah to be ready for the next term of federal court there and soon to be instituted against some Caldwell County people; that he had written this to the Princeton lawyer, but had in no way mentioned our client's name and had no information to justify such connection.

This information, immediately communicated to the banker, calmed his fears and caused him to conclude that the charge suddenly made against him was a mere ruse to surprise him into making some statement throwing light upon his business in our hands. Those with whom he was disputing were no more desirous than he to make the trouble public. Their counsel had been true to them and, as to this matter, had left the Princeton lawyer in the dark; but we had learned that a private settlement of this dispute was now impossible.

The Hollowell actions, one for each member of the family, could not now be filed too quickly, and as soon as requisite preliminaries could be met, this was done, and process was placed in the hands of a deputy United States marshal who was informed as to where the defendants—twenty-eight in number as now remembered —were to be found, and served without delay.

There were, we were told, seemingly a hundred or more in the band of assailants, but only those actually recognized by our clients were named as defendants. And these included different classes, from men of substance and high standing in church and community and prominent officials of the Association, down to the dregs of rural society. Though still confident of their strength and especially of their influence with the jury, some of whom might come from their part of the district, the defendants and their friends were disconcerted. Service of a summons in the name of the president of the United States to appear in a county outside their own, before a court whose officers they could not dominate, was a shock. Excitement was intense. Night Rider partisans in town and country boiled with rage. We perhaps did not adequately appreciate the unreasonable, undiscriminating nature of their hatred. We could not understand why the country's courts of justice should be closed against a part of its citizenry, or why a lawyer's life could be endangered by his advocacy of the cause of clients who were known and admitted by all to be the victims of an indefensible, unprovoked, and infamous outrage, when they pointed out their assailants and claimed redress. We did not feel conscious of the danger our friends seemed to apprehend. A similar band had not at that time hung up an able and highly respected lawyer, Captain Quinten J. Rankin, by the neck and riddled his body with bullets in a nearby Tennessee district for daring to represent interests adverse to the alleged rights of some members of the community. So we went quietly on with our practice.

After our Princeton client's fears had been allayed, we had made some progress with his private business before the Hollowell suits were filed. But immediately after the deputy marshal had gone to Caldwell County with the process, it became necessary to make a trip to Linton, Indiana, to see a man who held two notes for large amounts which this banker had signed for the promoters with whom he was now disputing. Princeton, on the way, was reached on a local train soon after dark and in time for a conference with him before the arrival of a through train with a sleeper for Indiana. He had grown so cautious as to ask that the larger hotels be avoided, and that our conferences be held at a less conspicuous place, and even there he had not met me in the lobby or dining room, but meals were served in my bedroom. He had not been told to expect me on this evening, as it was easy to call him after arrival. But while writing my name on the register, I noticed the clerk step into a telephone booth as if in answer to a call, and speak into the mouthpiece and say in a low tone, as I understood, "He is here." I suspected that he meant me, but said nothing and went to my room and had scarcely taken off my coat to use the wash bowl, when there was a knock at the door, and hardly waiting for the word, "Come," my client and two friends, closely connected with his bank, entered. He was breathing hard and apparently much excited. Heedless of the invitation to be seated and while all remained standing, he said:

"Mr. Miller, you have had important business of mine in your hands for several weeks, and have repeatedly been seen in private consultation with me at the bank and elsewhere, and also with my brother and me together. We three met a stranger [the Indiana man] in conference at a hotel. The business does not concern the bank. Even the bank directors and others are curious about our meetings. People are gossiping. Now you have brought suit for these Hollowells at Paducah, and people think that that is the matter we have been conferring about, that I am their friend and am backing them in this litigation—I am charged with it—the excitement is awful, and with you doing legal work for me that is secret, and the defendants in those suits threatening me, I am in danger and don't know what to do."

He paused as if for breath, and one of his friends said:

"Yes, Mr. Miller, the situation is critical—more so than you suspect. You have been in town barely more than thirty minutes, yet you have been spotted by at least fifty men. This room is being watched at this moment. Every time you have entered that bank for weeks, it has been like a live wire touching people all over the county. Our president is in a serious situation. Mr. —————— [the other friend present] and I came here with him because we were afraid for him to come alone to your room."

I assured the two gentlemen in the most positive language at my command that the man whom they thus escorted had been as ignorant of my intention to bring the Hollowell suits and was as innocent of any connection therewith as they themselves were, and that my business with him was of an entirely different kind.

"But," he broke in, "people don't know that, Mr. Miller."

"Then," I answered, "shall I take some papers from my pocket and show these gentlemen where I am going on your business tonight?"

He replied, "I prefer you should not make that business known."

Then I asked what he would have me do, and the same friend intervened again saying, "I think I understand matters, now, so as to assure people these suspicions as to any connection with the Hollowell matters are unfounded," etc.

But while saying he could so control the excitement as to save my banker client from danger, he left no doubt that the situation in other respects remained critical. My client desired me to proceed with his business, but still agitated, said the tobacco people were furious, that the Hollowell suits against them could accomplish nothing—they were going to charter a special train and come to the trial at Paducah, five hundred strong. "They will arrest that woman on the charge of scraping a plantbed, bring her here and put her in jail, then will tear down the jail, take her out and kill her. A million dollars would not induce me to sign her bond. For God's sake! Mr. Miller, won't you tell those people what I say and then dismiss those suits?"

I replied, "I will tell them just what you say, and if they then want the actions dismissed, it will be done. If they want to proceed, I shall stand by my clients, if your people shoot me into a thousand pieces." They left.

No one seemed to desire my society in the hotel office or dining room that night. The place was by no means attractive, and, thinking to have a chat with an old acquaintance, the Presbyterian minister who lived not far away and who opposed the Night Rider methods, I paid my bill and sallied forth. Early hour as it was, all places for business or pleasure seemed closed, the unlighted street deserted and silent. Finding the manse closed and dark, I did not knock. Informed now of being watched, and having my grip in hand, I did not return by the same streets but passed on to the railroad and down the track to the station and felt decidedly easier when the train had arrived and I was in the sleeper.

Returning from Indiana, I stopped for conference with our clients in Evansville. Robert Hollowell was out at his work but his wife and son were at home, and the former was promptly and impressively informed of the banker's opinion and advice. She unhesitatingly directed that the actions proceed vigorously, but desired that the delivery of the warning to Bob be left to her.

That warning, to do the banker justice, seemed honest, and his fears, in part at least, were not without foundation. Circumstances, seen later, indicated the purpose of the Silent Brigade to follow in the case of Mary Lou Hollowell the course his warning had marked out—since the suits had been brought despite the pending indictment.

The attack upon the Hollowell home in the spring of 1907 had seemed a shining success and produced for a time the desired effect. Opposition to Association plans, and to Night Rider methods was crushed. No one had been indicted for the open outrage. Not even an investigation by a grand jury, nor by any officer of the county or of the judicial district had been seriously attempted, nor, apparently, so much as seriously contemplated. The Hollowells were gone—Mary Lou indicted for a felony so that she dared not return to go before a grand jury, even if ever in future a fairly impartial grand jury should be possible. The danger to her would keep Bob away even had he in any case dared to come.

The same circuit court in which solemn charges that outlawry be investigated by the grand jury—the court which could have brought but did not bring before it Mary Lou Hollowell from McCracken County in 1907, to answer the indictment against her—also had power to bring her, her husband and son from the same place before a Caldwell County grand jury to tell that body the names of the men who committed the assault, but did not do *that*—though such course would have looked far more like a real effort to ferret out the facts than the most sonorous charge in the most solemn juridical tone.

The same cause that in 1907 prevented the arraignment of Mary Lou as an alleged culprit, prevented the bringing of herself, husband and son before an inquisitorial body as witnesses. The Night Riders were in complete control of parts of the county. Though they were a minority, the courts were prostrate before them—Princeton practically at their feet—bankers, merchants, editors, and professional men in the county seat, with some exceptions, were sworn soldiers of their cause, and the exceptions, fearing the torch, the lash, and the assassin's bullet, kept silence before them.

Some of the defendants in the Hollowell suits were residents of the adjoining county of Lyon which was in a different judicial district from Caldwell. But Night Riders dominated a greater portion of the former than of the latter county. Moreover one man of transcendent influence—politician, farmer, and eminent church member—clearly the county leader, was an ardent advocate and spokesman for the Black Tobacco Association and a bulwark for the Silent Brigade. Still the venerable county judge, the Honorable Lewis Crumbaugh, and the young county attorney, Walter Krone, did all they could to check lawlessness, the latter, as before stated, sustaining a public beating for his zeal. He finally changed to a residence in another state.

No adequate, if any, condemnation of the outrageous assault upon the Hollowells appeared in the columns of the local newspaper at Princeton. The citizens and authorities of the county were not urged to discover the perpetrators of the outrage; but a large number of the citizens of Princeton and vicinity, rushed into the columns of that paper in defense of those whom the victims, without any probability of a mistake, had named as their assailants. For the purpose of molding public sentiment in favor of one and against the other party in purely civil, individual law suits, a list of prominent citizens published, in the organ referred to, a signed "statement in reference to Caldwell County defendants in the Hollowell damage suit case at Paducah . . . certifying that for many years we have known (naming parties) defendants in the cases of Mary Lou Hollowell and her husband against them, now pending in the Federal Court at Paducah, Kentucky," and, after giving high praise of the defendants, continued, "that we believe they are wholly innocent of the charge brought against them by the Hollowells, and that they are in every way honest and good people, and as citizens of the good Commonwealth of Kentucky we deem it our duty to so certify to the world."

It may occur to some that the "citizens of the good Commonwealth of Kentucky" ought to have felt it their "duty" to make some effort to find out and "certify to the world" who did commit this crime that disgraced their own county.

As appears in the publication, a copy of which I still possess, the first to sign this certificate of the law-abiding character of these defendants and of his belief in their innocence was my client, the bank president, who a short time previously, had expressed to me his strong belief, that Mrs. Hollowell, if the actions were pressed, would be placed in jail at Princeton, and that "they will tear the jail down and take her out and kill her," and who so feared their fury that a million dollars would not induce him to sign her bailbond.

This certificate was signed by the president, the cashier and assistant cashier of each of the two National banks of the town, by the county judge, county attorney, county clerk, circuit court clerk, the commonwealth's attorney for that judicial district, mayor of the town of Princeton, chief of police thereof, county superintendent of schools, and other county officials, two Baptist ministers, by doctors, lawyers, and numerous others. Some of the signers were near blood relatives, some brothers-in-law or otherwise related by blood or marriage to some of these defendants, but that was not made to appear. The further fact that some of these county officials had taken upon themselves the obligation of the Night Rider oath and knew all the signs and signals of the order was not so well understood as it later came to be. A minority organized for lawlessness had terrorized the community, and some who signed this statement did so, doubtless, because of overpowering fear.

While such an unwarranted and socially hurtful effort to influence the course of public justice might be condemned, it is not mentioned here for such purpose, but for the purpose of showing the odds against our clients. Not only were they more obscure, less known throughout the federal district and even in Paducah, than some of the defendants, but they were almost totally unknown in Caldwell, their native county, outside of Princeton and the Night Rider hotbed in which they had lived till driven out. This publication by the officers and many leading citizens of that county not only plainly implied that they deserved to be driven out, but was a practical charge, under the circumstances, that they swore falsely in verifying their petitions seeking to recover damages against their neighbors who had always stood so high.

Doubtless, some of those signing this sweeping condemnation of the Hollowells in advance of any hearing, found it hard to believe in the guilt of some of their old business associates and acquaintances who had previously been examples of good citizenship and who now solemnly denied the charge made against them. Whether or not those who made this publication were all willing to "certify to the world" that all the defendants were equally incapable of the charges made against them, the certificate operated as a defense for all alike—precisely as if each signer knew each defendant and vouched for his innocence. The fact that the county and district officers, whose duty it was under oath to investigate, should sign such statement would seem to give it something almost akin to a judicial sanction. If it should turn out that these officers knew or could have known who the guilty parties were and took no steps to point them out, it only shows the madness of the strife.

But in such things "like produces like." People opposed to Night Rider methods, hoping for no lawful help, no court protection, prepared to protect themselves. It was said that some law-and-order clubs were formed for defense. Homes became small arsenals, Winchester rifles, shotguns, pistols, and ammunition found readier sale than at any time since the Civil War. It was said that panic was at times produced in Princeton by the rumored approach of Hill Billie bands at night to burn the town or to give some leaders a dose of the medicine Night Riders had forced down the throats of those who dared to oppose their course. But no Hill Billie bands attacked, and no outrages were committed by them. Still, from sheer necessity for self-protection, on the highways and in both public and private places, men went armed. The danger from this situation was well illustrated by an encounter between two well-known young men, Henry Wilson and Orbie Nabb. Both were popular. Nabb, from the south side of the county, was said to be a Night Rider captain. Wilson, though then living in Princeton, was from the north side and belonged to the opposite faction.

One night in March, 1908, while excitement over the pending Hollowell suits was at the boiling point, a traveling troupe gave a show at the Henrietta Opera House in Princeton. Wilson was one of the custodians of the building. Just what precipitated the collision I do not recall, if I ever knew. But upon going down the stairway after the close of the entertainment, Wilson met Nabb who was going up. Both were armed. Weapons were drawn in a flash. A pistol shot sounded, and Nabb tumbled to the foot of the stairway, dead. Wilson dashed for safety, found a horse and was soon in the Bethlehem neighborhood, seven miles away, among the homes of well-armed friends.

Fierce though the resentment rose and raged in

Princeton, Wilson was not pursued, and after a brief wait for preparation for his family to follow, he went to another state. Nabb's funeral was the occasion for a demonstration in the county seat by a vast procession in behalf of the cause for which he was considered a martyr, and resentment rose high; but Wilson, still only half a dozen miles distant, was not apprehended, though he was charged with murder, and, when the grand jury met, promptly indicted. Each faction now seemed to stand glaring in fury at the other.

The condition that prevailed in Caldwell County, prevailed over a great part of the Black Tobacco Belt. The lawless methods of building up the Association, forcing farmers by violence to pool their tobacco or cease to produce it, had now been followed for three or more years and, especially since the open Hollowell outrage, had passed without punishment or even legal investigation; outlawry had grown greatly in extent, in boldness and atrocity. And the oath-bound organization had assumed to regulate the behavior of all classes in all things whether they were related to the tobacco market or not. For instance, witness the destruction of the negro cabin and the murder of some of its inmates because their presence was not desired by some of the residents of the village of Birmingham in Marshall County; witness the stripes laid upon the back of the police judge of Eddyville, who has already been mentioned.

With the exception of the attack upon Princeton and the burning of the factories there, all the acts of violence that have been herein specified, occurred after the victory over Bob and Mary Lou. Many more could be named. No man knew when some secret foe might point him out as undesirable to the leaders of the tobacco organization and bring a band under Captain This or Colonel That to lay on the lash, or if resisted, take his life. As one red-bearded McGregor said to me, "A man feared to lie down at night without a loaded shotgun in reach under the edge of his bed." More than ten years after 1907, a close-mouthed, orderly citizen whom I had supposed to be a member of the Association, held up his crippled hand to me and explained that it resulted from a bomb placed in a stove in his store in a Night Rider neighborhood, because of his attitude during this stormy period. He had had the satisfaction of holding up that hand when his vote was solicited, a short time previous to our conversation, by a candidate for office, and of telling the candidate he could not vote for one who had advocated such methods.

Men in one part of a county feared those in a different part. Neighbor suspected neighbor. Openly or secretly the bulk of the Black Patch people were armed for conflict. Since about the beginning of 1906, town after town had been raided, building after building burnt or shattered. Fire insurance, bond and loan companies had withdrawn from the district. A few months prior to the time of the present writing a gentleman of Clarksville, Tennessee, who was warehouseman for the Association during Night Rider days, told me that he had in his warehouse in Clarksville, at one time, five thousand hogsheads of tobacco without a dollar of insurance of any kind, protected, he said, by his hired armed guards, day and night, against attacks by Hill Billies; and fearing for his personal safety, he went armed at all times during this period. No doubt he followed the only safe course open to him as protection to the property in his charge. And while the conditions which made it necessary and which had caused insurance companies to stand aloof, had been brought about by Night Riders and not by Hill Billies, the whole of the Black Patch was in a ferment of excitement and of antagonistic factions which placed life and property in imminent danger. There had been clashes between organized bands of Night Riders and the militia in some of the very few places where there had been, by this time, any attempt to invoke military force. Even in such a place as Paducah, prior to the spring of 1908, exceedingly disquieting reports of preparation for the raiding of the city by Night Riders had been received, and serious, well-grounded apprehension was felt for the safety of the large tobacco warehouses there. One step further in the march of organized lawlessness would have subjected Paducah to the same fate as Hopkinsville, Russellville, and other places which had suffered from raids and incendiarism. With few exceptions there was not in the whole Black Patch a Kentucky county in which, in a state court, and before a jury of that county, a Night Rider charged with an offense against a Hill Billie could have been convicted, or a Hill Billie charged with an offense against a Night Rider could have been acquitted. There were entire judicial districts in which this rule applied without a single safe exception. Practically military rule prevailed but the military was the Silent Brigade.

This was the situation as the three Hollowell suits came on for trial in the federal court at Paducah in April, 1908. The victims of the assault were the only witnesses to identify the assailants—practically three against thirty. Moreover each defendant was sure to bring with him one or more witnesses to corroborate his testimony and prove that he was elsewhere at the moment of the attack. It was said about that time that the outfit of a Night Rider on a raid, consisted of his "weapons, a mask, and an alibi." Thus approximately sixty or seventy witnesses of good standing would be brought to contradict the three plaintiffs, who were fugitives in another state and practically strangers in the city and county where the trial of each was to be. Moreover, a hundred and fifty miles of distance separated them and their attorneys, making consultation, selection of witnesses, finding of evidence, etc., difficult—to say nothing of the extreme danger of attempting any visit to the scene of the outrage to learn the facts. Then, under the Kentucky Code of Practice as to competency of witnesses (Sec. 606) which prevailed, it was thought by almost all lawyers up to that time, that neither husband or wife could testify for the other in such action as this. We thought otherwise, and though our junior member found one Kentucky case, sustaining our view, we thought it a dangerous point. It might be that in the case of the husband or the wife we would be reduced to two witnesses, as to substantive evidence, or have to face a difficult question on appeal if we should win below. The little boy's case was plainly of much less importance than that of either parent. Princeton, and all that part of Caldwell and Lyon counties, where alone witnesses might be found, was hostile ground. The neighborhood which was the scene of the outrage, a stranger must not enter. Some itinerants attempting to sell some articles were taken up, whipped, and forbidden to reënter the vicinity. It was thought one of plaintiff's attorneys visited even Princeton at the risk of his life.

We saw the difficulties and felt the responsibility confronting us, knew the defendants had employed exceptionably able counsel, and we determined to enlist, if possible, assistance for ourselves. Our first choice was Mr. Patrick H. Darby, whom we knew to be one of the ablest attorneys in the state—a lawyer without fear and without reproach. He was at that time a resident of Princeton and had for a lifetime been intimately acquainted with the citizenry of that county and of surrounding counties; he had his office in the same building and on the same floor with that of the Night Riders' local lawyer, saw them or their friends daily, and was in a position to learn all the facts of importance to our cases, which were possible for an outsider to learn; and he was more able than any other man in the native county of our clients to arouse some moral support for them.

I went to Princeton and asked him to join us in the cases. He declined for the sole reason that the interests of other clients—including his children and a railroad company whom he had long represented (some of whose property had already been burnt)—would be further jeopardized. The elegant residence that had been the home of his deceased wife would in all probability go up in smoke, should he appear as co-counsel in our cases and increase the hatred he had already incurred in these things. About as far as a man could be from sensationalism or braggadocio, he calmly said he had made up his mind that if men of these bands attempted to whip him, they would have to kill him. Such incidents will show the state of men's minds at that time.

We foresaw that in all probability more than one jury would be summoned, and though the first would consist of citizens of the Black Patch, the second, called expressly to try our cases or one of them, would come from elsewhere, partly at least, possibly, from Louisville, two hundred and twenty-seven miles away. So our next choice for co-counsel was the Honorable George Du Relle of that city, ex-judge of the court of appeals and onetime chief justice of Kentucky, but at the time United States district attorney, the duties of which office would in any case require his presence at the coming April term at Paducah. He agreed to assist us, and from that time we had his invaluable help.

Even in Paducah, anxiety increased as the court term approached, and nerves were strained to a higher and higher pitch till the feeling was intense. The fears before mentioned had been felt much earlier than the time at which these actions were filed. Now as the time for the trial came on, meetings of lawyers and citizens were held, as we were told, to prepare for emergencies. One prominent official was said to have expressed the opinion that I was in danger of being hung. We did not attend these meetings, but solicitous friends furnished us arms until our residence in Paducah as well as that on the farm, fifty miles away in the Bethlehem neighborhood near Princeton, occupied by us jointly with my brother and family during summer, was each furnished with Winchesters, pistols, and shotguns galore. But at Bird Place in the country it was pretty lonely at times, especially when two of us would be away and at court. Certain belongings were taken to the home of a neighbor thought to be safer from attack than ours. But the little family on the deeply shaded porch at night would hear the tramp of horses approaching in the distance. Lights out at once; and when a rendezvous of riders were found to be gathering where different roads came into the vacant lot around the old church at the foot of the hill in front, all at home crept into the stonewalled basement, where the one man armed with a repeating gun and others at hand, placed himself at a window facing the approach. There he waited until the band of horsemen formed in silence, and, but for the sound of marching hoofs, passed like specters on their way. It was later learned that these were the movements of a sort of patrol guarding that part of the county between Princeton and Fredonia against further Night Rider attacks.

One lawyer friend in Paducah brought me first a big pistol, and soon afterward a sort of old-fashioned hunting knife and scabbard to be worn concealed—the most villainous looking weapon imaginable. We ourselves were not so uneasy. We knew that the intense hatred borne by the defendants in these suits and by partisans of theirs against us, was well understood, and that if harm befell us in any way, however secret, suspicion would at once point to these defendants, who were now vowing to heaven and the public that they were law-abiding citizens. Just at this juncture, they would not court further suspicion. We felt this to be some degree of protection, for with all their bluff and bravado, they were obviously beginning to be slightly nervous, about what might sooner or later happen to them in the United States court. They had long proceeded under the belief—doubtless by advice of their local attorneys—that the federal court had no jurisdiction over them. Indeed, it had no criminal jurisdiction except for offenses against the laws of the federal government; and the fact that in all the Night Rider outrages it was impossible to discover with certainty any infraction of these laws would indicate legal advice in all they had done. And the courts of the United States, however oppressed one of its citizens might be by the lawless acts of other citizens of his state, even to the extent of shutting the state courts against him, could afford him no civil redress until he would forfeit his citizenship therein, and become a citizen of a different state. That such an oppressed citizen might become a citizen of another state for the express purpose of bringing a civil action in the federal court, seemed not to have occurred to the legal advisers of the Silent Brigade.

While the more prominent court officials and the leading business people of Paducah were opposed to the Night Riders and in sympathy with our clients, we learned for a certainty that there was in considerable classes a strong undercurrent to the contrary, and in communities within easy striking distance there were organizations that might well be feared. By some arrangement of which we were not informed—doubtless between county and state authorities—a company of state guards arrived and went into camp at Paducah immediately upon or very soon after the convening of the court. As soon as the district judge, the Honorable Walter Evans, was informed of this, he warned that soldiers must not attend the court, nor men in military garb be seen about the courtroom.

While Night Riders did not charter a separate train and come in one body, five hundred strong, as had been predicted, large numbers did come from Princeton on the Sunday afternoon preceding the opening of court, and others continued to drift in from counties in the Pennyrile and counties in the Purchase, so that by the time our cases were reached on the docket, Paducah contained far more than five hundred embittered partisans of the defendants, who had not by any means come without a purpose. And after all our watchfulness, we were surprised to find certain influential citizens of the city quietly but actively against our clients.

The plaintiffs did not dare take the usual, quick, convenient route by rail through Henderson and Princeton, nor even risk a boat trip on the Ohio from Evansville to Paducah, but took a roundabout way through Indiana and Illinois to Brookport on the north side of the river, crossing on a ferry boat on which they were met by two men especially employed to guard them from the wharf to a private boarding house, carefully avoiding notice as far as possible.

Though the authorities in Caldwell County had omitted the issual of a warrant to the sheriff of McCracken County for the arrest of Mary Lou Hollowell during her residence in Paducah for several months in 1907 after the indictment had been returned against her, now, inasmuch as she had the temerity to sue Caldwell County citizens, a warrant in the hands of the sheriff of McCracken County awaited her arrival, with the hope, doubtless, in the minds of the defendants that she would be unable to give bond for her appearance in the Caldwell Circuit Court. In that event, perhaps she might be quickly conveyed to the Princeton jail, or if not, she would be forced to pose as a guarded criminal while pressing her claims for damages in federal court. Instead, the sheriff who was ignorant of her arrival, was promptly informed that she awaited him in our office on Monday morning. There the warrant was served, and bond was signed by a citizen of Princeton, who was there for that purpose, and all the defendants hoped for from that maneuver was gone. It is extremely doubtful that there was another man in Princeton at that time who would have signed that bond. As matters now stood, not only was our client untrammeled. Before she would have to appear in the June term of Caldwell Circuit Court to answer the indictment, the defendants themselves must immediately face a court and a jury that did not fear them so abjectly as they had hitherto been feared. Moreover, this court could call an extra term, and they might have to attend a second or even a third trial before they could be sure of immunity and vengeance. True, it was impossible to reach them by indictment for a criminal offense in the United States court. But in the civil actions now pending they must meet the charge of a trespass *vi et armis*, and upon a judgment against them therein, a capias could issue for their arrest and confinement in jail if they should fail to pay the damages awarded. Unless this had been carefully explained by their counsel, it was probably not fully understood by the bulk of the defendants. But they realized that the facts of the shameful outrage at their very doors and hearthstones would be told in open court, and that while most of them upon cross-examination would have to admit they were aware of the assault at the time it was being made, they took no steps to assist the helpless victims and made no effort to detect or bring to justice the outlaws who branded their very homes with suspicion and shame. This was inconsistent with their ardor for law enforcement evinced in prosecuting Mary Lou for the alleged destruction of a plant-bed. Further still, the series of raids and crimes committed in Lyon, Marshall, Crittenden, and the northern part of Caldwell, civil redress for which was not yet barred by limitation, and the raid upon the Hollowells were obviously traceable to the same source. Moreover, Bennett, Rucker, Carden, and others could adopt the tactics of these plaintiffs, and a series of suits in the courts of the United States might follow. The outlook was serious.

All could readily see that interest in the impending legal combat would be intense. The whole strength of the Association, its partisans and adherents throughout the Black Patch, was enlisted—much of it drafted. The great majority of its membership consisted of those who were, ordinarily at least, good citizens, church members, homekeepers who "slept o' nights." Far less than all belonged to the so-called inner circle, or were actual Night Riders. But this better class was the real strength of the movement. They winked at, countenanced, even encouraged the outrages and shielded the culprits. Men in country and town who could not have been induced to volunteer in a lawless raid, took the Night Rider oath and knew the secret signals for use in the courtroom and elsewhere. They realized that in the beginning the tobacco grower was not the oppressor but the oppressed, and they not only sympathized with him as a neighbor—often as kinsman—but even when engaged in other callings, they were bound in a close community of interest with him and their prosperity depended on him. Not only did they cite ante-Revolutionary precedents, but their ethical and political theories were the same as those of the underground railroader who entered into a conspiracy to defeat and defy the Fugitive Slave Law, the same as those of John Brown, hung for treason in 1858 but lauded yet throughout the North as a martyr. At the same time the demagogue and cold-blooded trickster, holding official position or fattening upon salaries, perquisites, and often upon the use of funds such as he had never before been permitted to control, directed the affairs of the organization and labored to promote conditions which he had found so profitable.

The terror caused by these conditions was such that men feared to testify to facts which they knew, even under the protection of the United States court. They dreaded what might befall them upon returning to their homes. Strong men who had been summoned as witnesses came to our office and begged, some of them with tears in their eyes, that they should not be placed upon the stand as witnesses for the plaintiff, though they could state nothing unfavorable to the defendants. Some of them knew bits of fact which in certain contingencies might be of some corroborative value to plaintiffs. One man in particular admitted to me his knowledge of a fact which he did not suspect of being valuable as evidence. When told he could not be excused, his terror was obvious and manifestly sincere. He stated his belief that his life would be forfeited by testifying against the defendants, and said he would deny on the stand the statement he had privately made to us. He lived in Princeton. He was excused and the defendants probably never knew he had been summoned. He was a man of excellent reputation but lacked the physical and moral courage to face such an ordeal. Nor was he the only one to take this course; while others whose names our clients had given could not be found for service of a subpoena, and still others who had been so served were in sickbeds when trial day came. It was therefore hard to bring witnesses even to establish slight corroborative facts and circumstances. Not one person who had to return to a home near where the assault occurred dared to testify for the plaintiffs and then live in the midst of the defendants.

The defendants met no such hindrance. Their witnesses, free from any fear except that they might fail to show sufficient swiftness and alacrity in telling their story, were prompt to respond when given an opportunity. County officers, such as the county attorney of Caldwell, justices of the peace, even ministers of the Gospel, bankers, merchants, doctors, men of all classes came with apparent ardor to the help of the defendants. Their friends were not only active as lobbyists in and about the courtroom and corridors, as already stated, but on the street they tried to stir public sentiment in favor of defendants and cast odium on the plaintiffs. They caused to be placed in the hands of a petty Paducah bailiff a warrant from Caldwell County for the arrest of one of plaintiff's witnesses who had just come from that county, charging him with a misdemeanor alleged to have been committed long before, but for which he was now for the first time to be apprehended. In the midst of the trial the witness worked his way through the crowded courtroom to plaintiff's counsel, and whispered information that he was threatened with arrest. It was amusing to witness the trepidation and hear the asseverations of the little bailiff when brought in from the corridor to face the court and explain his action. The witness felt no further fear. The story behind all this will presently be told.

The three cases were to be tried separately. The first to be taken up was that of Robert L. Hollowell. He identified all the defendants except one, and named the man who applied the lash—a near neighbor he had known from boyhood. The one man whom he could not say he had seen among his asssailants was a kinsman and an exceedingly important leader and officer of the Association. Nor would his wife testify that she recognized this man on that occasion, but their son, Price, was certain he saw this relative among the assailants, and swore to that fact. This man and all the other defendants, each for himself, swore positively that he himself was not present, had no part in it and no information as to the names or identity of those who made the attack. But the defendants admitted that they took no steps to learn who the culprits were; and though some of the defendants lived within a few hundred yards of the plaintiff's home, heard all the volleys of firearms and uproar of the night, and knew who was being attacked, and though some of those nearest in distance were relatives—one of them a brother of plaintiff—none went to inquire, even after the tumult and the shouting died, as to what had befallen plaintiff, and were unable to explain why they did not, even on the next morning, try to learn if their smitten neighbor and kinsman needed help. He was so quiet and inoffensive, none could claim an offense or grudge against him—unless it had been his refusal to pool his tobacco. That they were not just now disposed to urge as an explanation, though he had sworn that such was the reason given for the stripes at the moment they were laid on.

But the character of Mary Lou, who had testified for her husband, was fiercely attacked, numbers of allegedly disinterested witnesses joining the defendants in swearing to a knowledge of her reputation and pronouncing it bad. This was done, partly of course, to destroy the value of her testimony, but mainly to make her prominent as the power pressing the litigation, bring all the three cases into bad odor, and by innuendo awaken in the minds of the jury the belief that the purpose of the assailants, whoever they may have been, was to run a base woman out of the community, and that she was now seeking damages and revenge against innocent parties who had incurred her hatred by their frank disapproval of her conduct. A swarm of hangers on, whisperers, and partisans of the Association, apparently tried to load the atmosphere of the trial with such an odor.

It can therefore be seen that it was not easy to find witnesses in the circle of plaintiff's former neighbors and acquaintances who could say they knew Mary Lou Hollowell's reputation prior to the time of this litigation and who would dare to contradict the defendants' cloud of high-standing witnesses and say that her reputation was good. Four such were found, three of whom were ladies of unimpeachable character who had known and associated with Mrs. Hollowell in Princeton, and one was the strong and prominent man who had signed her bailbond. All four said unhesitatingly that her reputation was good. The three ladies were members of families of the Fredonia Valley north of Princeton, though then living in that town. Other than these four only one witness for plaintiff outside his family is now recalled. He was Sanford Hall who had been threatened with arrest; and as the scene, already mentioned, in which the little bailiff stood before the court had been enacted in the presence of the jury, all were keen to hear what he had to say. He was an ex-Night Rider. The facts he stated were only circumstantial and corroborative, but in their setting could not well be denied, and were difficult of any explanation consistent with the innocence of the defendants. These had claimed they did not know until the suits were instituted that they were even suspected of complicity in the assault. But the testimony of Hall who had been one of the inner circle, showed that on a certain afternoon prior to the time the suits were filed, in a meeting in a schoolhouse at which he was present, these defendants had met the counsel now representing them in consultation, each bringing his witness to establish his alibi in preparation for a trial that was to be held at Paducah, McCracken County; and that at a time still earlier than this Caldwell County meetings, they had, in addition to their local attorney at Princeton, employed special counsel for this trial. For when asked how defendants knew to prepare for this trial in this court even before the suits had been filed, he said that the attorneys they had employed in still another county and in a town seventy-five miles away, which he named, had sent them word, and had then come at an appointed time, for a conference with clients and their witnesses. The fact of this meeting could not be denied—if any had chosen to deny it—for the strange visit of distinguished lawyers from another county to a small schoolhouse in a remote corner of Caldwell County, reached only after a journey of seventy-five miles, ten or fifteen of which were traveled in horse vehicles over miserable mud roads in winter, had not escaped notice. The jury now caught the significance of the effort to intimidate Hall. He was unlearned, obscure, and charged with some misdemeanor, but little use was it to attack the character of a witness whose testimony could not be denied.

It was said that Hall's brother, ——————— Hall, had been suspected by the Night Riders of being an informant against them. Certain it is that he mysteriously disappeared. It was said that he went to the bottom of a natural well, or pit, in an out-of-the-way nook with a stone tied to his neck. It was from Hall that we first learned the name, Silent Brigade, the Night Rider oath, challenge and countersign, courtroom signals, names of the different colonels, captains, and much of their procedure and methods; and it seemed undoubtedly true that many were literally forced to join the inner circle. You may be sure Hall did not return to his old haunts. It was perhaps arranged for him to join the regular army under a different name.

As each defendant denied any part in the attack, he could not say whether any other defendant was guiltless except in the instances where two defendants claimed to be together at a different place. So, in the main, each brought a witness who was not a co-defendant. But the alibi effort was overdone. It looked suspicious for each defendant to bring an alibi witness, not a party to the suit, and to prove just where he was and what he was doing in the "wee sma' hours" on that particular night, a year before, when neither he nor his witness had any thought of ever being called to testify to the fact, and had nothing to impress it upon his mind. The residences of defendants covered a considerable area—some were miles out of hearing distance of the firing—some in Lyon County. Counsel for plaintiff in argument, and the court afterward in his charge, called the jury's attention to the remarkable fact that in this farming community, during the strenuous season, when people worked hard through the long days and used and needed to use the short nights for sleep, people throughout that area should have happened to be awake at precisely the same late hour on that particular night; that seventy of them a year afterward, many of them with nothing whatever to impress it upon the mind, could tell just where they were and what they were doing even down to most trivial particulars; and that each of the numerous defendants should have happened to be in company with some one awake like himself, and able to remember precisely enough to swear he was not at the scene of the trouble. Yet these people in every part of the neighborhood, the jury was reminded, on all roads and approaches, some distant and out of hearing of the tumult, others so near as to hear even the voices of the assailants and see the flashes of firearms, and all wide awake, could tell nothing to show what direction the lawless band of possibly one hundred came or went. Apparently a troop had dropped from the sky or risen through the earth, and with force and arms and loud tumult destroyed a home, and then as suddenly and mysteriously disappeared, and, apart from the wrecked building and bruised, bleeding victims, "left no mark or trace behind." True, an ardent partisan had seen a mounted troop on that night passing through the village of Wallonia in Trigg County, headed toward Caldwell, but none of the seventy witnesses had seen such band in the vicinity of plaintiff's home or any horse tracks in the road next morning.

One of the most positive—even belligerent—of the alibi witnesses was a justice of the peace "in and for Caldwell County," who had spent the night at the home of one of the defendants, his brother-in-law, near plaintiff's home, and in hearing distance of the attack. This witness admitted that he and his brother-in-law and family were up and passing about the house and yard, heard the firing and tumult and knew it was at the house of the plaintiff, but did not go nigh nor make inquiry after all was quiet; and the next morning, this sworn conservator of the peace and member of the county government set up no inquisition nor made the slightest effort to learn whether or not the furious fusillade against plaintiff's house had resulted in death or injury to any one, but calmly mounted his horse and rode away.

Counsel on each side of the case were orderly and polite, indulging in no offensive "flings"—were evidently conscious of the grave situation and of their responsibility. The court was rigid with dignity but very alert. For though perfect decorum prevailed, the crowded courtroom at times as the trial and interest grew intense fairly quivered with that suppressed excitement whose silence means much. People pressed up close where they could, some crouching even on the steps of the judge's stand. On tiptoe in the corridors they strained ear and eye to hear and see all they could as the struggle neared a climax. And they were not idlers, merely hungering for sensation. Public-spirited men of the city and from the county throughout the Purchase and the Pennyrile, had caught the significance of the occasion, and lent their quiet but impressive presence. The large number of the earnest partisans of the defendants from far and near had come for the one purpose of attending the trial, and formed the greater part of the audience. They hung as closely as they were permitted upon the flanks of the jury, and watched the movements of its members at each recess. The struggle between Constitutional Government and Organized Lawlessness had reached a crisis. In the forum of the nation relief was sought against oppression in the state. The test was more important to the Black Patch public than it was to the plaintiffs who sought redress of personal wrongs. "When leagued Oppression" ruled the courts of the state, all its living victims might yet find a tribunal that promised some redress.

Of various interesting incidents of the occasion only one or two more shall be named. At one time during the trial, a Paducah lawyer, shrewd in jury trial tactics, found a chance, though not connected with the case, to say to me: "You have a Night Rider on your jury." Then designating a certain man, he asked: "Didn't you see his agitation—how he sweat and squirmed when you were testing his qualifications?" We had certainly noticed it, and would have challenged the talesman but for the fact that our clients strongly urged that he be taken. In his young manhood he had lived in their county, and though he now lived in another, and was not in touch with them, they had a comparatively short time previously, been informed that he had expressed strong hatred for Night Riders, and they had been by these trusted informants so strongly impressed that they were rejoiced to see him accepted. We thought that as he was a respectable, amiable man, his agitation might result from dread of having to decide such a question between old neighbors. That man and one other hung the jury. Before many days I learned why, as will soon appear.

The fact that only two out of twelve jurors stood between them and disaster was an eye-opener for the defendants. And the fact that an extra sitting of the court was ordered for a day in the following month, May, 1908, for the one purpose, a retrial of this case—when the whole jury would probably be called from parts of the state beyond the reach of the Silent Brigade, could not have seemed to them a cheerful outlook.

To my great surprise, one day between the date of the first trial and the time of that to come, I received the following letter:

Augustus E. Wilson　　　State of Kentucky
Governor　　　　　　　　Executive Department
　　　　　　　　　　　　Frankfort
　　　　　　　　　　　　May 5, 1908.

Mr. John G. Miller,
Attorney at Law,
Paducah, Ky.

My Dear Sir:

I send you herewith a copy of a communication received by me. It is corroborated in a great many details by information from my secret service. I believe the man is writing the whole truth as far as he knows it. He is not interested in the case and I am not, and I merely send you this for your information. It need not be acknowledged, and it should be carefully guarded to avoid any danger to the life of the man who sends it, who does not give me his name, but gives me much useful information. The letter is printed with pencil to avoid detection.

Yours truly,
(Signed) AUGUSTUS E. WILSON

The copy of the letter to Governor Wilson is too long to be quoted here, and for obvious reasons the names of the persons it charges with criminal conduct must not be given. The letter begins thus:

4/30, 1908.

Hon. Augustus E. Wilson,
Frankfort, Ky.

DEAR SIR,—

I am a night rider, was put in under the gun. Men have been forced to join them just as they have been forced to join the association. When you join the night riders you are informed it is inside work of the association, that night riding is indorsed by the association and in fact is part of it.

Now I know the truth and I am going to tell it so help me God. ———— is a night rider because he wants to be. [The man named here held an office particularly important at that time.] He is in close touch with them at all times and ready to serve them on all occasions. He is using his office to defeat the law and encourage lawlessness. No question about this. The jury box has been opened and the men on both juries who were not inside were put in before they had any thought of being jurymen. Again do not put confidence in sheriffs, jailors or city marshals; they are treacherous; no guessing about this. You now know the condition of affairs. I ask what can be done? A perjured court, jury, county officials and witnesses. I would be glad to furnish you a list of some but it would be useless. . . . Now if you would like to assist the Federal Court in the Hollowell case, just listen at a night rider school house convention doing business.

 1st. Heavily armed sentinels take their places.
 2nd. Password taken up.
 3rd. House called to order by Captain or Colonel.
 4th. Speaker: "Gentlemen, we have very important business before us tonight. You all know about our Paducah case. Those men who are sued are fighting our fight. If they lose our cause is lost. We must win this case. To win it takes money, and ——————— (of ———————) the founder of our noble order has commanded that each member shall pay ——————— which is to pay witnesses and their expenses and pay attorney fees in this Hollowell suit. I am authorized to collect this money and turn same over to our Sect. Mr. ——————— for this purpose."

——————— you know is one of the defendants in the case . . . ; and all the night riders seem to know that ——————— ordered ——————— to shoot Mrs. Hollowell that night.

Much stated by this communication revealing supposed secrets was already known to us through sources of which its author could not know, which strengthened belief in its truthfulness. Our client had told us she recognized the man who shot her, a miscreant from another neighborhood, and this communication named the same person, but it was news to us that he had been ordered to do so by ———————, whom we knew to be an Association leader. This leader according to the informant was, with another, in joint command of the raid upon Princeton. And the informant's letter continued, "——————— led the raid (360) at Hopkinsville and was wounded (by his own men) behind the right ear. Was succeeded by Colonel ———————.

———— had charge of the men at Fredonia, ———— showing the way."

But most interesting of all was the light thrown upon the juror who in the first trial of the Hollowell case had been "spotted" by my lawyer friend as a Night Rider, and who, with one other, hung the jury for the defendants. The letter said: "———— (of ————) one of the jurors who tried this case, took the night rider oath ten days before the trial, and promised to hang the jury until hell froze over, regardless of testimony. So did the other juryman promise the same. ————, I think his name is. This oath was administered by ———— (of ————) and witnessed by ———— (of ————) and ———— (of ————)." Then speaking of the man who had administered the oath to the man who had been summoned for the jury, the informant stated that "———— says he was in the Hollowell raid himself. He also says he has administered the oath 900 times" etc.

The letter then explained the process by which the indictment against Mrs. Hollowell was obtained in a way that would seem incredible to me but for things which I learned at this time and some years later to be true beyond a doubt. "In this way," the letter concluded, "Mrs. Hollowell was indicted at Princeton and the night riders thought they were safe from prosecution as Robert Hollowell and wife could not appear against them without answering the charge against Mrs. Hollowell. I have heard this matter discussed in the Lodges exactly as stated."

The facts stated in this communication, which was carefully kept secret from the Hollowells and their witness, Hall, were so completely in harmony with what they told us it was impossible to doubt the story. Facts they gave us in private, which were not made public on the witness stand nor elsewhere, were also told in this letter by one of whom they knew nothing, and who could not have known what they had thus told us. This information was strikingly true as to the method in finding the indictment against the woman and as to the purpose of the charge laid at her door. The writer said he wrote at the risk of his life in case he should be suspected of spying, but offered to furnish further information upon certain conditions: one of which was that he was never to appear as a witness in court; another, a pardon for himself and certain colleagues, four of whom had joined the Silent Brigade through fear and "had done no violence"; and the final condition, "I must be protected financially and bodily if the situation should demand it." What further arrangements, if any, were made with him, I never knew. Nor did I ever learn who wrote this strange letter—some of the most peculiar statements of which are not mentioned here—but incredible as some of the statements may seem, I am thoroughly convinced that they are substantially true.

At the next sitting of the court, in May, 1908, called specially for a retrial of this case, a jury came from other districts of the state, and a verdict for $35,000.00 damages was returned in favor of Robert L. Hollowell, against all the defendants, jointly; judgment went accordingly, and *capias ad satisfaciendum* was awarded.

Steps for an appeal were taken but the appeal, not at once perfected, seemed to be held over us *in terrorem*. We declined to be terrified. The two other Hollowell cases went over to the November term. These, still pending, were more of a terror to the defendants than was their threat of appeal to us.

On the second trial the court declined to allow the wife to testify for the husband—or, possibly, we did not offer to introduce her as a witness. While this forced us to rely upon two witnesses, plaintiff and his little son, as to the main facts, it eliminated the only doubtful legal question, and at the same time relieved us of all necessity to defend the character of the wife, and left defendants' artillery for this attack upon her useless in their hands; and as the court had required us to prove that each defendant was not merely an aiding or abetting conspirator, but an actual participant in the alleged attack, and had charged the jury accordingly, the verdict and judgment were unassailable.

Still the combat, legal and otherwise, was fiercer on the second trial even than it had been at the first. The friends of law and order had, even in such places as Eddyville and Princeton, spoken out more boldly and the breach between the factions had widened. The defendants and their friends had held power till their arrogance hardly knew bounds, and to speak openly against their course, except in certain places, was to incur insult or maltreatment. On the other hand, some of those who had been forced to flee the state, came into Paducah and even taunted some of the Night Riders during the progress of these trials. But these did not venture into the region beyond the Cumberland. Conditions even in Paducah were strained at this time: One night when we were busy in our office, the telephone rang in our home. My wife answered and was asked if she had been disturbed, and she was told that a man had been seen prowling at our back porch and leaving over the rear fence. She had heard nothing, and was told to have no fear, as a guard would be stationed there. Promptly some armed militia took a stand near by. No further explanation was asked or given. But the residence was watched and guarded, front and rear, until the trial was over and the danger passed.

The defendants blustered and said that the judgment could never be collected. And it soon developed that all those owning property had long since executed mortgages, making it appear that, though they had been known and rated as financially sound, they were but a group of bankrupts. Few things showed more clearly the baleful influence and power of the organized lawlessness than did these mortgages, the bulk of which had, a few months previously been executed to and accepted by an institution, or the representative thereof, whose officers must have been aware of their fraudulent nature and purpose. And it was hard to be patient and polite when men ranking high in business intelligence came to us, as some such did, and with the utmost show of candor assured us of the practically insolvent condition of the defendants, made for them, and had the face to urge us to accept, an offer of compromise that was almost an insult to our own intelligence. One member of the deputation, sufficiently defiant and outspoken in other respects, took no part, it was noticed, in representing how destitute the defendants were. He said to me years afterward, that he would stand by his friends but would not tell for them a story which he thought we would not believe and which he knew to be false. He was in good faith a member of the Association. The others we knew to be its secret enemies but basely serving its purpose through abject fear.

These defendants had apparently become so drunk with their sense of importance and power they could not realize that the arm even of the United States could reach them on their native heath, or, if it could, that plaintiff or his counsel would dare invoke its aid. So after the lapse of proper time, when a United States deputy marshal, armed with a capias, appeared in their midst, and they actually saw that property was not to be levied upon, but that immediate payment or bond for full satisfaction of the judgment was the only means of escaping quick arrest and imprisonment to last until they should under vigorous examination explain to dispassionate federal authorities their financial condition and the cause for those mortgages, the consternation and the fury were extreme. Men swore and women wept. In addition, a large part of the country, including especially the business interests of two or more county seats, was violently agitated.

It took little thought to remember that not only two more Hollowell suits remained to be tried, but that these three actions had blazed a path that Bennett, Rucker, Carden, and various others might follow. Men and business interests throughout the Black Patch not only feared to refuse help to the Night Rider organization, but were in various ways so involved in its activities and identified by actual membership, willing or unwilling, that escape from its liabilities was legally doubtful, and often actually dangerous, if attempted. Hundreds beside those already sued might become defendants in similar actions. In distress, unscrupulous leaders might point out to the lawyers of prospective plaintiffs those who could be charged with complicity in one way or another in these lawless raids. Later events showed that these fears were well grounded. Would-be law-abiding members of the Black Tobacco Association were at the mercy of the lawless.

Strong appeals were made to the officer by defendants and even by some of plaintiff's friends for time to arrange for adjustment, and in compliance with urgent requests, I went the following day on a morning train to Princeton for a conference. The defendants and their partisans thronged the town, and occasionally, one of them would pass and scowl at me through the hall door of Mr. Darby's office, where I awaited their representatives; but for some reason, possibly to test our eagerness for compromise, my presence, which had been so urgently solicited, was otherwise utterly ignored. After waiting some hours, without the slightest comment or inquiry, I took the first afternoon train for Paducah, leaving instruction for the deputy marshal to execute his writ. As we were afterward told, panic came again. Certain it is that within a few minutes after my arrival at our office in Paducah at about five P.M., a long distance telephone call from Mr. Darby stated that Mr.

——————, a wealthy Caldwell County citizen, had come as a mutual friend and was then instructing him to say that the defendants very much regretted their blunder in failing to explain duly that they were waiting to determine how much ready money could be raised, that they were now ready with a sum certain, and begged that I would take the six o'clock train from Paducah to meet them and their counsel at Princeton that evening. This suggestion was declined, but they were told I was going to Evansville on the following day, could see their counsel within the hour between trains at Princeton, hear their offer, convey it to our clients, wire from Evansville if it should be accepted and receive payment upon my return through Princeton, the officer in the meantime holding up the writ. This plan was followed precisely, and upon my return trip, one of the defendant's attorneys awaited the train's arrival at the Princeton station, and handed me a certified check for the agreed sum.

Robert Hollowell had not recovered his nerve after his shocking experience, was still shaky and had been made more so by unfavorable reports sent him by people he ought not to have believed but did believe; he greatly dreaded the long delay of an appeal, protracted litigation over the mortgages and otherwise; he labored under a vague apprehension he could not himself explain, and was really eager for an adjustment. So when offered an amount sufficient to pay his lawyers' fees with all expenses and losses incurred, and leave a net sum sufficient to purchase—as he soon did—a far more valuable farm than that from which he had been forced to flee, he would brook no further parley or delay, but demanded immediate settlement, ending as this did, all the Hollowell Night Rider litigation. Moreover, the compromise was desired by many as a step toward a general peace in the Black Patch, and friends and well-wishers of the plaintiffs and of their attorneys had urged its consummation.

Meanwhile a number of suits had been instituted by *émigrés* from the Black Patch, following the lead of the Hollowell cases, but naming a much larger number of defendants. Then a sort of levy was made upon many who were not defendants. To illustrate: An Association leader active in the Hollowell and other cases, walked into the store of a merchant who was yet a defendant in none, and after a sort of survey said: "Mr. N————, you should, I think, pay so much to assist the Association in certain cases and you have been so assessed. You will be called upon in a few days to pay it." N———— paid it when called upon soon afterward. This man was one of three, made defendants in later suits, who sought to employ Miller & Miller to make defense for them. They were citizens of high rank and were doubtless innocent of culpable complicity in any lawlessness; but agreement as to a fee was not reached, and they decided to share with many others the burden of a compromise —one of them paying, according to report, $1,000.00 as his individual contribution.

It was commonly reported that when well-known adherents of the Night Rider organization would be named in some of these actions, a sort of tentative compromise agreement would be made upon condition that the plaintiff's lawyers would join as defendants other solvent and well-to-do citizens designated by those already sued. Certain it is, that after a compromise conference between the counsel of plaintiffs and leaders among the defendants with their counsel in some of the most important of these actions, amended petitions were filed and numbers of new defendants were sued, and afterward called upon to carry out a compromise of the original making of which they were totally ignorant. Thus leaders in the movement and those against whom lawless acts could be proved levied contribution on others, many of whom were truly innocent, and saved themselves from imprisonment and financial ruin, the murderous thug escaping with the rest. Thus innocent men, willing or unwilling members of the Association, knew that unscrupulous co-defendants would gladly implicate them in shameful outrages, and finding themselves between two fires did not dare to make defense.

Some members of the legal profession were tempted into unbecoming practices. Two young lawyers from a town of considerable size came to our office in Paducah, and asked us to join them, as counsel for the plaintiff, in a suit in federal court in which about one hundred and fifty persons were named as defendants in the pleading laid before us. We at once pointed out the names of persons known by us to be opposed to the thing with which they were therein charged—some who had assisted us in hunting evidence in our cases, and some who had consulted us in these matters. They promptly agreed to strike these names out if we would accept employment against the rest. But we wanted to know what evidence there was for a cause of action against the main body, and ran through the list, pointing out other names and inquiring for proof. It was then frankly admitted that there was little or no proof against any except a very few of those named, but that this list had been given these young men, and that almost or quite all of these proposed defendants would each pay at least a small sum to avoid the expense and vexation of employing counsel and making defense, to say nothing of the danger they would apprehend from an action in which we would assist the plaintiff in that court. Of course, the employment was declined. But this will show the extent to which the evil had reached.

Other than that for the Hollowells, our firm brought no action for damages against the Night Riders except one for a poor frightened creature named Stephens, who as he claimed had been forcibly made a member of the organization. He claimed that its membership, fearing he had become a witness against them had kidnaped him from his home, and taken him one night, several miles to the pit that was said to have swallowed young Hall, with the avowed purpose of casting him into it. He said they had begun fastening a heavy stone to him, but under his piteous begging and the intercession of one of his captors he was warned and released. The story leaked out, and the county attorney of Lyon County, in which Stephens lived, taking a squad of militia, followed the trail from Stephens' home finding by tracks where the band had crossed a creek at a certain place in the woods and had passed other points he named till the pit in a secluded place was found, and by it a stone with fencing wire attached, and the ground trampled and marked by tracks of men and horses. But Stephens and his wife, who had found refuge in Paducah, were well nigh insane with fear; and before the time of trial, mysteriously disappeared, and what became of them we never could learn.

Another interesting incident connected with these troubles was that in the suit brought by Bennett against a number of persons for their assault upon him; a prominent lawyer and former state senator was named as a defendant. It was said that Bennett, contrary to the advice of his own attorneys, had caused this lawyer's name to be added as a defendant. When court came on, counsel for the plaintiff, upon the earnest representation of this prominent man, and with the kindest of feeling for him, caused the action as against him to be dismissed without prejudice.

To the great surprise of Bennett's lawyers, two of whom lived in Louisville, one in Paducah and one in Marion, Kentucky, the ex-senator instituted in the Lyon Circuit Court an action for malicious prosecution, making Bennett and all four of his lawyers defendants, and praying $50,000.00 damages. But as none of the defendants resided in Lyon County, that court could have no personal jurisdiction of them without service of process upon at least one of them inside that county. Under the Kentucky Code, service upon one of them in the county in which such transitory action was pending, gave the court jurisdiction of all who might be served in any county in the state. The sheriff of Lyon County boarded a train, when it stopped at a station in the county, and served summons upon one of these defendant lawyers passing there on this train—perhaps the first information these defendants had of such action.

Here again the services of our firm were called for. A trial of that action in such a Night Rider hotbed as that town and that county were then known to be would not only have meant a certain judgment for the plaintiff in large damages, but none of the defendants cared to assume the physical risk of attending such trial there as this would surely be. There was good ground for such fear. Bennett's attendance upon the trial of this case in the state court in Eddyville at that time would have been courting certain death. The town and surrounding community were already aquiver with rage because of the presence of a small detachment of militia sent there by the state's governor at the request of the county judge and county attorney, before referred to.

Members of the Silent Brigade about as well armed and well drilled as the few raw militia stationed there would have come from all directions in great numbers to such trial; a clash between such forces would have been inevitable, and in it Bennett would not have been the only victim. It was but too evident that the only purpose in making the four lawyers defendants to this action was to give the state court jurisdiction of Bennett, who had become a citizen of Illinois, make sure a judgment at Eddyville where evidence would count for little in his behalf, and if he dared to attend and testify, it would serve only to give opportunity for his foes to wreak physical vengeance on him. Further, if he dared to appear in Paducah to prosecute his action in the federal court for damages against those he accused of having assaulted him, personal service upon him would be easy. The one hope for him and his four co-defendants to escape disaster was a removal of this action from the state court at Eddyville to the United States court. Our firm was then employed, and one of its members, unaccompanied by any of the defendants to the action, appeared on the first day of the following term of the Lyon Circuit Court, filed a petition in behalf of Bennett for a removal and having a power of attorney, executed the necessary bond, entered motion for removal, presented and argued grounds therefor. The presiding judge promptly overruled the motion, but the state of the record was such that the action did not stand for trial till the next term, about four months away. Within that time a copy of the whole record had been filed in the court of the United States, and an injunction had been applied for and granted, restraining the state court from further action till the United States court could hear and pass upon the application for removal. When that time came, our view—which was that the cause of action stated against Bennett was separable from that alleged against his co-defendants—was held to be correct, and the action against him was held to be removed, and that against the others was remanded to the Lyon Circuit Court. But no further prosecution of the action against Bennett in the one court nor against his lawyers in the other was attempted. People were left to speculate upon the curious ending of this litigation.

It remains to be said that after a time bitter quarrels

broke out inside the Night Rider brotherhood. One of the prominent defendants in our Hollowell suits, who for some reason was assaulted, shot and badly wounded in his home by former confederates, removed to a different state, just as the Hollowells had removed, and brought his suit against his alleged assailants in the same court in which they, the Hollowells, had sued him and some of the same confederates. While our firm had no connection with his case, I sat, a spectator in the courtroom, and heard him on the witness stand fully admit that he had taken part in the assault upon Robert L. Hollowell and family, and expressly admit that he had committed perjury in that witness box when he swore to the contrary on the two trials of the Hollowell case.

Omitting numbers of incidents connected with the story which might have been interesting, I have now given the main, outstanding facts of this strange episode in Black Patch annals. After the institution of the Hollowell suits, aggressive Night Rider activities as against those outside of the organization, had, by the time the first trial came on, practically been abandoned. And I cannot recall a single open raid occurring after the first trial, or mistrial, of one of these actions in April, 1908. Those involved in the various suits brought against themselves or their friends by victims of Night Rider lawlessness were soon very busy trying to meet these demands for damages already claimed. Some of them were not devoid of a sense of humor. It was said that two young bloods of the mask and alibi fraternity met, casually, and one said, "Haven't seen you lately. What're you doin' these days?" The answer was, "Plowin' corn for Mary Lou."

Old grudges lived, it is true, and secret vengeance was sometimes inflicted, the torch and the bomb covertly applied, here and there, and serious damage done. And the vicious influence of the unlawful organization which has been described was still active, where it dared to be, was plainly effective upon courts and juries for several years longer in such places, and perhaps has not yet entirely disappeared. It will not die with the generation that saw its birth.—"The evil that men do lives after them."—But when it was seen that the power of the United States could be invoked, though only in civil damage suits, by victims of the Silent Brigade, the boast, "We fear no judge nor jury," was no longer heard.

Still it will doubtless seem strange to some that such victim in this latter day, though a citizen of the nation, could not call upon the court of his nation to protect him in his home, which for centuries the Anglo-Saxon has proudly called his castle. Nevertheless, it was, as it yet is, true that the national government which could tax him for its support or draft him into the army for its defense could not help him defend his castle or the life of himself or his family therein. If his castle had been burnt by his fellow-citizens and he and every member of his family had perished in the flames, the United States government of which they were all citizens would have been powerless to punish the murderers. When because of local conditions the state government utterly fails to protect, as it did in the Black Patch, and the

United States government is powerless to protect the citizen in his home, what remedy for the evil is to be provided? When a struggle between a devilfish, capitalistic Trust, on the one hand, and a labor or industrial confederation, no less a Trust, on the other, in a conflict of monopoly against monopoly—class against class—regardless of the public weal, brings social chaos, riot, and bloodshed over wide scopes of the national domain, or when a great city is terrorized by a game of incendiarism, bomb-throwing, and murder between rival factions struggling for control and making local self-government a shame and a menace, why should the Constitution, when a call comes for protection of the citizen by the United States government, make it necessary for the nation's attorney general to answer, as the present attorney general has more than once been constrained to answer, that such intervention by the national sovereignty would be unauthorized and that the request must be denied?

NOTE

It may be well to say that this monograph was written during the closing months of 1927 and the early part of 1928, so that it may be seen that the last sentence of the text could not refer to any conditions or official acts of a later date.

As the records of the District Court of the United States for the Western District of Kentucky will corroborate the statements made of the facts in the cases of the Hollowells, Bennetts, and others as showing the conditions in the Black Tobacco Belt at the period named in the text, fuller documentation is not thought necessary. These and the records in the state courts of Caldwell, Lyon, and other counties in that section are open and may be examined by all who wish.

The record of the indictment of Mary Lou Hollowell for scraping a plantbed and that against Henry Wilson for murder may be found in the office of the Caldwell Circuit Court—both having been dismissed as each of those persons was finally pardoned before arraignment for trial.

The original letter of Governor Wilson, dated May 5, 1908, and the copy of that from the confessing but anonymous Night Rider, which the Governor enclosed with his to me are both now in my possession, as is also a clipping from "Twice-a-Week-Leader" of Princeton, Kentucky, bearing the names of prominent citizens, about one hundred and twenty in number, who thus publicly came to the assistance of the defendants in the Hollowell cases. Those on this list who were civil officers, or officers of banks, etc., annexed their titles in signing.

J. G. M.

www.ingramcontent.com/pod-product-compliance
Lightning Source LLC
Chambersburg PA
CBHW030345100526
44592CB00010B/839